photo by MICHAEL LICHTER

photo by MICHAEL LICHTER

Indian Larry

Chopper Shaman

Dave Nichols *with* Andrea "Bambi" Cambridge
Photography by Michael Lichter

MOTORBOOKS

First published in 2006 by Motorbooks, an imprint of MBI Publishing Company, Galtier Plaza, Suite 200, 380 Jackson Street, St. Paul, MN 55101-3885 USA

© Dave Nichols, Andrea Cambridge and Michael Lichter, 2005

All rights reserved. With the exception of quoting brief passages for the purposes of review, no part of this publication may be reproduced without prior written permission from the Publisher.

The information in this book is true and complete to the best of our knowledge. All recommendations are made without any guarantee on the part of the author or Publisher, who also disclaim any liability incurred in connection with the use of this data or specific details.

This publication has been prepared solely by MBI Publishing Company and is not approved or licensed by any other entity. We recognize that some words, model names, and designations mentioned herein are the property of the trademark holder. We use them for identification purposes only. This is not an official publication.

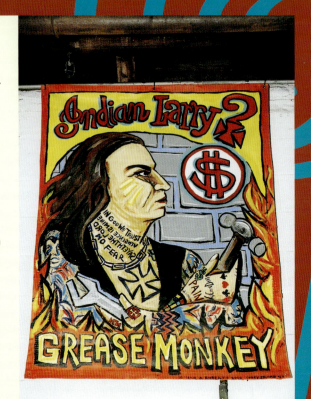

artwork by MARIE ROBERTS

Motorbooks titles are also available at discounts in bulk quantity for industrial or sales-promotional use. For details write to Special Sales Manager at MBI Publishing Company, Galtier Plaza, Suite 200, 380 Jackson Street, St. Paul, MN 55101-3885 USA.

ISBN-13: 978-0-7603-2382-3
ISBN-10: 0-7603-2382-8

Editor: Darwin Holmstrom

Designer:
Rochelle Schultz Brancato

Printed in China

Photography on the front cover, back cover, frontis and title page by Michael Lichter. Front flap illustration by Pat Redding. Index photo contributed by Andrea Cambridge.

photo by MICHAEL LICHTER

	Dedication 6
	Introduction: **The Chopper Hero with A Thousand Faces** 9
1	**The Daring DeSmedt** 16
2	**Rat Fink Freak** 26
3	**Rebel Without A Pause** 36
4	**Pri-Zen** 46
5	**The Biker Lifestyle** 58
	Chopper Gallery 70
6	**To Hell and Back** 96
7	**The Hero and the Goddess** 108
8	**Media Magician** 122
9	**Fame and Fortune** 136
10	**Legends Never Die** 150
	Index 176

Larry's close friend, photographer Timothy White on his Indian Larry bike. contributed by BAMBI

Photographer Michael Lichter and Indian Larry at Billy Lane's Choppers Inc. in Melbourne, Florida. photo by BOBBY SEEGER

DEDICATION

This book is dedicated to the life and spirit of Indian Larry DeSmedt, and to his friends and family. Most notably, this book is humbly offered to Larry's wife and soulmate, Andrea "Bambi" Cambridge, and to his close working partners and friends, Paul Cox, Keino, Johnny Mack, and Elisa and Bobby Seeger. You have all been incredibly generous with your time, I know it was very difficult to dredge up old memories of the man you all loved and respected so much.

Most of the family photographs of Larry from the time he was a baby, all they way through his amazing life, came from Bambi. I can't thank you enough dear mermaid. Special thanks go out to Larry's close friend, Timothy White for his stunning photography, and to my associate, Michael Lichter for painstakingly shooting all of Larry's wild custom motorcycles.

The book would not exist without my friend and gentle editor, Darwin Holmstrom at Motorbooks. Darwin happens to be a fan of Joseph Campbell and therefore, didn't think I was crazy when I proposed that Indian Larry walked step by step through the Hero's Journey in his fascinating life. Blessings go out to Dr. Jean Houston for her many years of Mystery School teachings, her wit, her endless hunger for knowing, her compassion and wisdom. I felt you guiding my words many times for "these are the times and we are the people . . ." Most importantly, boundless love and laughter fly to my dear

Paul Cox and Indian Larry: brothers forever.

photo from INDIAN LARRY ARCHIVES

Hanging with Jesse James at the Laughlin River Run.

contributed by BAMBI

wife, Diane. Just as Larry had his mermaid, I have my very own Tinkerbell. And much love to my son William, the warrior with the mighty spear. You two are my inspiration.

A word of caution to the reader: this is not a book that was created to exploit Indian Larry through detailed accounts of his darker nature or questionable acts in order to sensationalize his life. Those in search of such tabloid thrills would be best served to put this book down immediately and move on to more gamey material. Rather, this tome is a tribute to the very real man who became a living legend, hoping to explain how this came to be.

So let me take you by the hand as we go spelunking in forgotten caves of consciousness to reveal the hero that lives within us all. The way may be twisting and dark at times, but glories await us. Come, take my hand . . .

Special thanks go out to the following friends and family of Indian Larry DeSmedt for the photography in this book: Andrea "Bambi" Cambridge, Bobby and Elisa Seeger, Paul Cox, Keino, the DeSmedt family archives, Timothy White, and Michael Lichter Photography.

To contact Indian Larry Legacy call 718-609-9184, or visit www.indianlarry.com.

—*Dave Nichols, October 2nd, 2005*

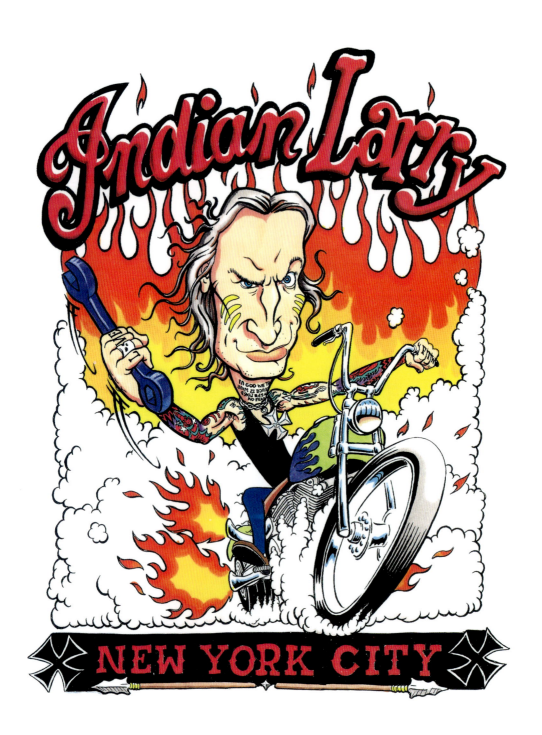

artwork by STEVE ELLIS

The Chopper Hero with A Thousand Faces

INDIAN Larry's life follows the pattern of a mythic tale. It is the archetypal story of a man with a thousand faces; an ordinary man much like you or me but whose life led him on an extraordinary adventure. In his time he was a jester-thief, a warrior-prince, a lover-king, a wizard-shaman, a sideshow enigma, an artist with metal, a stuntman, a mentor, a heroic celebrity, and much more. In his lifetime, Larry DeSmedt played every part and role in the human pageant.

Some of Larry's friends have said that he lived many lifetimes during just the one in which they knew him. In his time this man loved, traveled far, did great and nefarious deeds, and even experienced his own "death" and was reborn a new being. He became a man who lived in two worlds, both physical and spiritual.

To understand the man, it is important to understand the larger context and dimension of his life. It helps to think of Larry in the context of ancient Greek mythology—in which many lives were often lived in one lifetime, and that in all lives one life is shared. The work of Joseph Campbell, who defined the hero's journey in his book, *Hero with A Thousand Faces*, also brings to context the life of Larry.

Campbell maps out the way by defining the connective links in all great myths. In much the same way, Indian Larry's story is actually all our

Riding in for the taping of *Late Show with David Letterman*.
contributed by BAMBI

contributed by BAMBI

stories, writ large. For Larry DeSmedt lived both the life of the everyman and an epic life. He was both a man of the people and a bigger-than-life heroic character. Larry learned to activate his entelechy, a state of being in which a creature realizes its fullest potential. In Larry's case, this involved seeing himself on the stage of life as a total being; it allowed him to imagine his grandest vision, then turn that vision into reality. As the entelechy of the acorn is the fully realized oak tree in all its glory, Larry became a shamanic chopper builder, realizing his spiritual visions as mobile, mechanical sculptures. We all have the ability to realize our grandest visions on the stage of eternity, but few are bold enough to pursue that adventure.

Larry's heroic journey began with an average middle-American existence. As with all great stories and heroic journeys, something lurked below the surface of this snapshot of Americana. Larry's life was soon

Larry's "signature look":
wife-beater tank, sweatpants, and flip-flops.

Publicity shot for Larry's Coney Island gig.

contributed by BAMBI

thrown out of balance. Like anyone in this situation, Larry spent much of the rest of his life trying to restore the normalcy of his early life. Naturally, this never happened, for when the old life of normalcy is washed away, a true hero ultimately becomes more than he could have ever imagined. He is literally reborn to a new life. It is by meeting life's challenges that a hero achieves entelechy. The greater the challenges, the more fully the hero realizes his or her true nature, and Larry's life was a filled with great challenges.

As Dr. Jean Houston says in her book, *The Hero and the Goddess*, "I believe that all great stories have powers encoded in them that can help us change our lives, and by changing our lives, change the world—for the better, one hopes." So it is with Larry's life story. In it we see our own

Would you let this man kiss your baby? or
Hanging out behind Choppers Inc.

photo by MICHAEL LICHTER

life's path, the ups and downs, tragedies and wonders. We see ourselves descending to Hell and being reborn anew. The most important function of a mythic journey is to foster the centering and unfolding of the individual in integrity. This is done within the hero (the microcosm), the universe (the macrocosm), and within the great mystery that transcends both.

Heroes tend to emerge in a time of dying. Death may take the form of one's self, society, religion, government, relationships, and so on. The hero's life is first thrown out of balance. He is then asked to answer the call of the eternal and step into his role as hero. This requires undergoing a gestation process, often through trauma, growth, and ultimately rebirth into a new form. Often, the second great task for the hero is to return to the world. This is the shamanic journey, bringing back the wisdom gleaned in the adventure to the tribe. In such a fashion, Jesus returned from the desert, the Buddha returned from his meditations, the great Odysseus returned from his years of voyaging. In our modern myths, Dorothy returned to Kansas from Oz a transformed being. Luke Skywalker helped Darth Vader return balance to the force (prophesy fulfilled), and Neo, from *The Matrix*, merged with the source (resurrection) to create a new world view (program).

During the mythic journey, the hero nearly always falls from grace, traveling through a dark night of the soul before being reborn anew.

Larry seen here with his long lost brother, Earl the eel.

contributed by BAMBI

Checking out a familiar profile during the Laughlin River Run in Nevada. contributed by BAMBI

Indian Larry's life journey took him through such dark nights, ultimately hitting bottom in every sense of the word. As with all classic tales, he also had magical helpers who offered magical gifts and learning, which helped the hero move on. Many great stories include a sacred marriage (often to a true goddess), and in Larry's case, he married a mythical character: the mermaid.

Before we begin the journey of life as seen through our friend, Indian Larry, let us look at the classical hero's journey as summarized by Joseph Campbell. Drawing upon hundreds of examples of this journey as seen through all great mythic tales, Campbell offers a synopsis of the hero's journey as it is experienced in myths around the world:

> *The mythological hero, setting forth from his common day hut or castle, is lured, carried away, or else voluntarily proceeds to the threshold of adventure. There he encounters a shadow presence that guards the passage. The hero may defeat or conciliate this power and go alive into the kingdom of the dark (brother-battle, dragon-battle: offering, charm) or is slain by the opponent and descends in death (dismemberment, crucifixion). Beyond the threshold, then, the hero journeys through the world of unfamiliar yet strangely intimate forces, some of which severely threaten him (test), some of which give him magical aid (helpers). When he arrives at the nadir of the mythological realm, he undergoes a supreme*

photo by MICHAEL LICHTER

photo from INDIAN LARRY ARCHIVES

ordeal and gains his reward. The triumph may be represented as the hero's sexual union with the Goddess—the father-creator (father-atonement), his own divinization (apotheosis), or again—if the powers have remained unfriendly to him—his theft of the boon he came to gain (bride-theft, fire-theft): intrinsically it is an expansion of Consciousness and therewith of being (illumination, transfiguration, freedom). The final work is that of return. If the powers have blessed the hero, he now sets forth under their protection (emissary); if not, he flees and is pursued (transformation flight, obstacle flight). At the return threshold the transcendental powers must remain behind; the hero reemerges from the kingdom of dread (return, resurrection). The boon that he brings restores the world (elixir).

As we enter the amazing life of Indian Larry, we will attempt to peel away some of the layers of enigma that surrounded the man, the myth, and the legend. We will learn of his love for custom hot rods and

photo by MICHAEL LICHTER

motorcycles. Trace his short career as a bank robber. Join him in the belly of the beast during his time in prison. Witness his spiral downward, his dark night of heroin addiction, and his hitting bottom before being reborn in 1994 as the very spiritual bike builder who has become a hero to many.

It is no mistake that Larry used the question mark as his personal brand. As Larry himself said of his question mark logo, "That's my life's logo because I don't know what's going on. Roll with the mystery, life is uncertain . . . just be comfortable with that. Why fight it?"

And so we begin this mythic tale, appropriately enough, with many questions. Who was Indian Larry? Why did his life profoundly change so many others? How is it that this man seemingly lived so many lifetimes worth of human experience in a too-short 55 years? Why was he taken from us so early? Wheels within wheels, questions within questions. What better place to begin?

Larry test riding Jesse Jurrens' recently built *Low Life* in Melbourne, FL.

The Daring DeSmedt

"Larry lived his art, there's no doubt about it.
His life was his art."

TIMOTHY WHITE, *Larry's close friend, photographer.*

IMAGINE a land of infinite possibility. A place where neighborhoods were safe, where science was providing better living through chemistry, where a boy could grow up and truly believe in something called "the American Dream." The horrors of World War II were fading, the economy was booming, new inventions were bursting forth everyday to make your life better. Everything was very clean and you could buy a hamburger for a nickel. Gasoline was cheap, cars were more powerful, and a new thing called a drive-thru restaurant meant you could eat and drive at the same time. Life was better than good; it was miraculous. It was into this idyllic and very mythic American landscape that Lawrence DeSmedt dropped on April 28, 1949, in upstate New York.

Unlike many classic myths, Larry was not born holding onto the ankle of his evil twin, nor was he born from a virgin birth or from some strange mating with various water fowl. Larry was born to mother

photo by DAN HOWELL

Larry was always attracted to the thrills and spills of the carnival life, eventually receiving stunt training from Wall of Death pro Sam Morgan.

Larry riding Rhett Rotten's Wall of Death.

photos from INDIAN LARRY ARCHIVES

Dorothy and father Augustine, and later had two younger sisters, Diane and Tina. Larry spent his early years in a home his father, a second-generation carpenter, built with his own two hands.

As is the case with many great hero stories, Larry was born a common man among the people, as opposed to a member of an exalted family or royalty; he was born into a situation that the average person can fathom. This made him the perfect everyman and sets the stage for the hero he will someday become, along with the rocky journey that led to that point. For the DeSmedts, America was truly the land of opportunity. In the great melting pot that is New York, people from every nation, faith, and creed could join together under the banner of liberty. In the 1950s, America still honored some of the declarations of independence set forth by its forefathers.

Even at a young age, Larry showed signs of being interested in building things and had a very artistic nature. He loved Lincoln Logs, those wonderful kits that came in a big round tube, offering various cut and painted wooden pieces for making log cabins and the like. Larry would build cabins, tear them down, and build them again over and over. He also discovered plastic model kits at an early age.

Do you remember the smell of airplane glue and Testor's paint? Do you remember carefully moving model car pieces back and forth, back and forth, until they broke off from the rest of the pieces? Do you remember filing the little nubs off of the parts and pretending that you were actually building a full sized custom hot rod? I sure do and so did Larry. His favorite model kits were those put out by Revell of Ed "Big Daddy" Roth's too cool custom cars with names like the *Beatnik Bandit* (1960), *Road Agent* (1961), *Rotar* (1962), *Druid Princess*, *Mysterion* (1963), and *Orbitron* (1964).

Lawrence DeSmedt was born on April 28, 1949, in upstate New York. He was a happy baby.

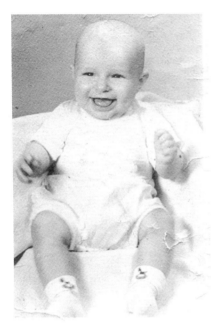

Larry built them all in excruciating detail. He was amazed that a guy like Ed Roth could make a living by drawing wild creatures such as Rat Fink and Surf Fink, make T-shirts out of them, and build innovative hot rods and custom motorcycles. You could say that the die was already cast with young Larry. Naturally, Larry's dad wanted him to become a carpenter and carry on the family business tradition, but Larry was always more outgoing and imaginative than that particular path allowed one to be. "He was a good boy, but mischievous," says his mother, Dorothy.

Larry liked drawing monsters and hot rods. He liked watching *The Addams Family* on TV or going to see the latest Roger Corman cheap-o monster movie at the local drive-in. These movies included *It Conquers the World* and *I Was a Teenaged Werewolf*.

For a young lad growing up in upstate New York, the kustom kulture scene that was happening in California must have seemed like a wonderland. Here was a place where it never snowed, where all the girls were tan and wore bikinis, where an industrious young moto artist could make a fortune doing what he loved. No doubt, these kinds of thoughts led Larry to take apart his sister Tina's tricycle and strap a lawnmower engine to it. You could say that the customizing bug had bit Larry, and he never looked back.

To discourage Larry's rebellious streak, Augustine sent him to a very strict Catholic elementary school. As you might imagine, the original wild child did not take well to nuns with rulers. As Larry himself said,

photos from DeSMEDT FAMILY ARCHIVES

Larry and his sister Diane at a kiddie park. From his scowl, it looks like Larry didn't dig it too much.

Young Larry ready for school in a time before schoolyard shootings.

Eight-year-old Larry endured the strict "domination model" of the Catholic School to a point—then rebelled even more.

"I was raised Catholic, so they completely destroyed me." In our current enlightened age, we know the last thing you want to do with an inventive young mind overflowing with artistic ability and imaginative thought is strap it to a desk for eight hours and force it to regurgitate facts and dates that it will forget a few days later. At any rate, the strict Catholic school experience only fanned the fires of Larry's rebellious nature, and very soon the DeSmedt family found itself with a Tasmanian devil on its hands—the fire of Larry's rebellion became a raging inferno.

Larry's surviving sister, Tina Wells remembers: "Larry and the Catholic school did not do very well. He would come home with bleeding knuckles (no doubt from being rapped on by savage nuns), and mom would say, 'What happened?' Larry would just say that he got into a fight."

It's interesting to note that the original model for our modern school systems was aimed at doing one thing: create young people who could fit perfectly into the cogs of society and work in the many factories that were created at the beginning of the Industrial Revolution. America needed worker bees who did not question authority. Clearly, Larry was not one to be pressed into a preconceived mold.

The seeds of contempt germinated within Larry. He'd seen films such as Stanley Kramer's *The Wild One*, a fictionalized depiction of the Hollister Riot of 1954. He could relate to Marlon Brando's biker character, Johnny, and Lee Marvin's bawdy Chico. When asked what he was rebelling against, Larry could well respond as Johnny did: "Whaddaya got?"

Sure, all kids have a rebellious streak, but Larry tended to take things a step further, even as a kid. One day, filled with angst about the cruelties of his school, Larry went to the basement of his house and

photo from DeSMEDT FAMILY ARCHIVES

Larry's mother and sister Tina with him and Grease Monkey.

constructed a crude, homemade bomb. His hope was to do some damage to the Catholic school, maybe even shut it down for a few days. Larry didn't want to hurt anybody, but the hero within him imagined that by shutting down the school for a few days, he might be seen as a savior by his peers at school. He was more interested in justice and liberty than revenge.

Not being a professional bomb maker, things went terribly wrong. The makeshift bomb blew up, blowing off the pinky finger on Larry's left hand. Imagine his parents' horror, imagine Larry's terror, and imagine going through the rest of your life with four fingers on your left hand. However, years later, Larry was philosophical about the accident: "Like most horrible atrocities that happen to you in life, when you look at them in retrospect, it's usually a blessing or a lesson. It's not much fun when you're caught up in it, but it's better. You can get into tighter spots . . . makes you a better mechanic." And that was true, Larry could indeed reach into places that no normal, five-fingered man could.

This particular chapter of Larry's life taught him one profound lesson. Larry was a complex individual who often saw life's pageant on a broader scale. He was capable of seeing the big picture, as if watching his life on the big screen. The movie of Larry's life fascinated him and he was always curious to see what the next scene would hold. It was just a matter of laughing things off. Larry was truly bigger than the events in his life; he rose above them every time.

In the great myths, the hero at some point separates from the reality he has known and grew up in. He receives the call to adventure and often is presented with a heraldic gift of sorts, which changes his perspective. In a way, Larry's mishap with the homemade bomb acted as that twisted gift. In a land of five fingered boys and girls, he now stood

photo by GRACE MARTINI

out. It would be up to Larry to decide if this gift would make him a freak or an avatar.

As he entered into his rebellious teenage years, Larry saw the America he grew up in change for the worse. Politicians were lying to the people, a war in Vietnam was forcing young men to their deaths in the rice patties of South Asia for a cause they didn't understand. The wonder of television brought the horrors of war right into the living room every night. Timothy Leary was telling young people to drop acid and drop out of school and society: "turn on, tune in, drop out." College students shouted "peace, not war," and in a supposed land of the free, war protesters at Kent State University were killed by our own National Guard. It seemed that the American dream was over.

Larry would soon hear his own call to adventure.

Rat Fink Freak

"When I die I want to meet God
and say, 'What the hell were you thinking?'"
INDIAN LARRY

IT can be said that, for each of us, the wounds of life become the catalyst for the emergence of a new life. The difficult times of our life often define us. After all, a person never really knows what he or she is capable of until he or she encounters significant opposition. In all great myths and legends, the hero emerges in a time that marks the end of one form of life. As noted earlier, heroes often emerge in a time of dying, be it in the form of a death of one's self, society, religion, government, or relationships. The hero's life is first thrown out of balance. He is then asked to answer the call of the eternal and step into his role as hero. This requires undergoing a gestation process, often through trauma, growth, and ultimately rebirth to a new form of being.

In the fascinating true-life story of Larry DeSmedt, wounds took many forms in his young life. Just as the Fisher King of the Holy Grail myth suffers from wounds that never heal, so Larry suffered permanent wounds. And, as with the Grail King, the land and the King in Larry's phantascape were often one and the same. He was psychologically

contributed by BAMBI

photo from DeSMEDT FAMILY ARCHIVES

scarred by the nuns at his high school. He was spiritually scarred by the failure of religion to live up to his broader view of reality. He was emotionally scarred by the lies his society, government, and country told. And, he was physically and mythically scarred by the accident that took his finger and made him appear freakish to the regular world of "normal" citizens. In fact, Larry had a life-long love affair with the freak shows and "carney" life found on the Coney Island Pier. He could relate to the sideshow performers who didn't fit into the slick suit and tie of American life in the 1960s.

It is often wounds such as these that allow inner strength to rise up from the depths of despair, enabling the great source and spirit to make itself known in our lives. This is how the ordinary becomes the exceptional. It is also one of the ways in which the higher self, or oversoul, is revealed to us.

Consider Larry's sacred wound. The wounding acts to reframe life's cruelties on all realms. The gifts of such wounds include deep empathy for others. After all, one never really has empathy for others' wounds until one has suffered greatly himself. In Larry's life, this led to his own journey of enlightenment.

Larry soon encountered a series of initiations into the realms of his own depths. Initiations come in many forms and many of them are painful, which is why Larry had the word "PAIN" tattooed on his hand.

Larry found a balm for the wounds of his young life in the zany work of Ed "Big Daddy" Roth. Roth was out there, and Larry could relate to Roth's wild drawings of madcap, slobbering creatures in kick-ass hot rods and on custom motorcycles. Ed Roth turned the 1960s on its ear, borrowing from psychedelic counter-culture images and the very California kustom kulture scene that he devised, along with

Larry at Ted's V-Twin.

mind-melting painter Robt. Williams and blue-collar pinstriper Kenneth Howard, also known as Von Dutch. This turbulent trio would later play a huge role in Larry's life.

Larry's dream was to join such freethinkers in California and live the life of a radical designer, artist, and customizer. That opportunity materialized out of the ether when his younger sister Diane ran away from home at the age of 16 and moved to California. As a teenager, Larry plunged headfirst into the wild, hippie counterculture of booze, drugs, free love, and rock'n' roll that defined the flower-power generation. There's even a famous photograph of Larry at Woodstock. You can apparently take the boy away from the carney but never get the carney away from the boy, for in this weathered photo we see Larry, high atop a pole in the best "polesitter" tradition.

Besides the lure of hippydom, Larry had also seen an anthem of American youth of the 1960s, the film *Easy Rider*. Hollywood mavericks Peter Fonda and Dennis Hopper were hip to the avant-garde art, music, and drug scenes, and decided to create a youth film that would place a big road sign smack dab in the middle of human consciousness. It was 1969, a time of the death of flower power innocence. From the napalm

photos from INDIAN LARRY ARCHIVES

BILLY LANE

Choppers Inc., Melbourne, Florida

I first met Larry at Sturgis in 2002 at the Camel Roadhouse. I'd seen some of his bikes in magazines. I walked up to him and said, "Hi, Larry, I'm Billy and I really love your stuff." I kinda thought he might be an asshole or something but he was really nice; he was a humble, down-to-earth person—I didn't expect that.

When I think of Larry I always remember him working on carburetors; he was really gifted at tuning them, and worked on some of mine. I remember he would get this focused, determined look on his face, listening to the engine change as

photo by MICHAEL LICHTER

Motorcycles got under Larry's skin and into his blood at an early age.

he dialed in the bike. He would zone out and become totally immersed in tuning that carburetor, like it was his whole world. It was cool.

Larry was a jokester too. I remember one time he, Paul Cox, and myself were sharing a house in Hawaii and every morning I'd exercise and Larry and Paul would wade around in the ocean. We relaxed and talked, and just had a bitchin' time. Well, one morning Larry said to me, "Billy, come here." So I waded over to him, really close. He smiled and said, "I really love to pee in the ocean." He just started to laugh and he went on saying how there was nothing like taking a pee in the ocean. He was a character and a half.

One thing that always impressed me about Larry was how deeply he would think about things. He would have deep thoughts about things that you wouldn't expect. I always felt like he was swimming down at the deep end of the thought pool while I was wading in the shallow end.

Of all of my memories of Larry, one of my favorites was when we were hanging out at Sturgis just before he died. We were set up next to each other at The Full Throttle Saloon, just hanging out inside his really hot trailer, shooting the shit. I was drinking a bunch of beer and we were just kicking back.

I think if Larry walked into my place right now he'd say, "Hey, Billy, what's goin' on?" And if he *did* walk into my shop, I think I'd take him shopping for some clothes. Get him out of those sweatpants and flip-flops.

I find myself thinking about Larry a lot. We did a lot of public appearances together at the *Easyriders* Bike Shows

horrors of Vietnam, to the beating and killing of Kent State students, America's youth was primed and ready for *Easy Rider*.

Larry could relate to the misunderstood, chopper-riding bikers portrayed by Fonda and Hopper; he'd started riding customized motorcycles himself. The stage was set for Larry's call to adventure. According to his surviving sister Tina, "One month before he was to graduate high school he said, 'Mom I'm going to California.'" Clearly, the all-American importance conferred upon earning a high-school diploma meant little to Larry. He was, after all, the original wild child.

Often, when the hero leaves his traditional home, he finds himself descending into an unreal world, a land of fairies in the mythic realm. For Larry's surreal fairy kingdom, he chose the sandy beaches of southern California, mythic land of fruits and nuts. His sister Diane was already neck deep in the party world of drugs, and Larry soon followed suit. Drugs made him do a number of things that he wasn't proud of later, including robbing hippies to buy more dope. But through the blur of drugged dementia, a bright light awaited Larry. He met his mentor, Ed Roth—a huge deal for Larry. After all, Larry had lovingly put together every Ed Roth model kit Revell ever produced when he was but a wee

around the country and I remember that he was really good at dealing with people. We'd often talk about our rise in popularity and I remember he told me one time, "No matter how much something seems like it matters, it doesn't really matter at all."

We spent hours and hours signing autographs for people at bike shows and Larry could pull it off—he taught me how to chill out when stressed. We traveled every weekend together at the *Easyriders* Bike Shows, meeting people, taking pictures with them, and signing autographs for ten hours, non-stop. I'd get all stressed and then I'd look over at Larry and he would be smiling and signing some girl's ass or something, and I'd think, "This ain't so bad."

Today, you see Larry's influence everywhere in the custom bike world. You see a lot more people doing the twisty stuff that Larry did (twisting the frame down tubes or springer front ends). It's a tribute to Larry that people are doing that. While most custom bike guys were trying to hide all their cables and wiring, making everything look sleek, Larry let everything hang out in a raw, functional way. I always call Larry's style of bike the Brooklyn style. It's raw and hardcore, just like Larry.

The morning Larry went out for his last ride he told me something I'll never forget. He walked past my booth on the way out the door to do his stunt riding. He touched me on the shoulder and said, "I'll be right back." That was unforgettable.

—Billy Lane

"Ya should'a seen da other guy!" contributed by BAMBI

lad. Roth was said to have liked the young hippy/biker and recognized Larry's budding creative genius.

Larry entered Roth's world of cars and comics, sexy drawings of pin-up girls, and base humor. While Roth followed the earlier art of Von Dutch, it was "Big Daddy" who was the marketing genius, marrying hot rods with wild T-shirt designs and model kits. The combination placed Roth's work in the homes of people from all walks of life, all over the world. Big Daddy Roth became a counter-culture idol. On the custom car scene, many of his designs were controversial because he combined car and bikes together in such awe-inspiring vehicles as his V-8-powered *California Cruiser* trike (1966). After designing and creating over half a dozen of these hybrid vehicles, Roth was alienated from much of the current hot rod establishment. As such, many of his odd-ball trikes were

photo from INDIAN LARRY ARCHIVES

The members of the Polar Bear Club enjoy taking a dip in freezing waters.

banned from custom car shows. Roth just laughed about it, saying, "Isn't the idea to do something different?"

This would become Larry's credo as well. It is no accident that, many years later, one of Larry's favorite custom creations was the Rat Fink bike he built as a tribute to Ed Roth. This was the motorcycle that won Larry's first go 'round on The Discovery Channel's *Biker Build-Off* TV series.

In 1966 Ed Roth started *Choppers*, one of the first modified-motorcycle magazines. At the time, artist Robt. Williams worked as Roth's art director, and both men loved Von Dutch's work. *Choppers* ran an article on Von Dutch in one of the first issues. But Big Daddy soon grew tired of the politics of publishing and liquidated his assets. He took to hanging out with outlaw bike clubs. "We rode and had fun and everyone pretty much steered clear of us," Roth said. His hot rodding hedonism soon caused the Revell Corporation to terminate their contract with him. Interestingly, in the 1970s Roth, Williams, and Von Dutch united to work on Jim Brucker's famous Movieworld Cars of the Stars and Planes of Fame. The museum was a popular Orange County attraction until Brucker closed it in 1979.

The throbbing tornado of kustom kulture spit Larry out on the doorstep of *Choppers* magazine in 1969. One look at this magical land of motorized munchkins convinced him right away that he was not in Kansas anymore. Here, Larry connected with the gods of customizing and met his own heroes (another theme in every mythic life).

Within the adventure, a hero must pass many tests and trials to prove his worth. Larry was about to encounter a tragedy as profound and deeply wounding as can be suffered by mere mortals. He was about to transgress into the Shadowlands in earnest and enter the very belly of the beast. His first true descent into the netherworld was at hand.

photos from INDIAN LARRY ARCHIVES

artwork by PAT REDDING

Rebel Without A Pause

"The loss goes way, way deeper beyond the loss of the man. He [Indian Larry] was the guy who didn't sell out."

RUSSELL MITCHELL

THE early life of Larry DeSmedt was a mythic journey that began with his call to adventure, which took place when Larry blew off his finger with a homemade bomb. This curse was also a blessing in a way, since Larry's disfigurement helped keep him from getting drafted and away from war in Vietnam. It therefore allowed him to travel to California where his real adventure began.

This sort of blundering into the adventure often happens. In *The Odyssey*, the call to adventure begins when 72 of Odysseus' crew are killed by dismemberment. This is a common way for an adventure to begin; once the hero is sent to some far off land (a land very different from his own), he encounters strange and amazing things. This was certainly true for Larry in the land of hippies and free love that was California in the late 1960s.

As noted previously, in every hero's journey, helpers aid the knight or shaman on his way to complete tasks. These helpers are often supernatural beings, members of the faerie world, gods or goddesses, or

Larry probably wanted to steal a cop car since he was a kid.

beings who have already stepped over into the land of faerie and returned. For Odysseus, the very gods help him on his way as seen when Poseidon and Zeus blow his ships across the oceans for nine days to enter a threshold between worlds. For Larry, his beautiful sister Diane was one such helper. Diane, it turns out, was very familiar with the alternate reality that one can enter through psychedelic drugs.

However, at this point in a mythic tale the hero usually enters another land that can be a descent into hell or the belly of the whale. In *The Odyssey*, Odysseus and his crew land on an island and enter the cave of the Cyclops who intends to eat them. For Larry, the mythic journey to California became that dark cave, that belly of the whale, that bad drug trip.

Larry enjoyed the endless summer of California life. He walked the streets of Haight-Ashbury at the height of the hippy craze. He hob-knobbed with beat poets and drug dealers, musicians and artists galore. He met his idols, the gods of kustom kulture, and found himself in a heaven of his own design. In June of 1971, *Easyriders* magazine debuted, bursting forth on an unsuspecting world. Here was a magazine that encapsulated many of the things Larry loved: custom motorcycles, biker lifestyle, innovative art, and gorgeous women.

The nuns at Catholic school no longer shackled Larry. He was free of parental constraints and living life at full throttle. Larry probably later thought of his time in California as a four-year college course in freedom. This amazing era ended abruptly on June 21, 1971, when Larry's sister Diane was murdered.

There are no words for the emotional roller coaster that Larry found himself on, so utter despair will have to serve. He had always been a sensitive and artistic child, feeling more than most. Now as a man of 22

contributed by BAMBI

Always up for a good time, Larry does burnouts in a cop car somewhere near Amboy, California.

Yep, that's Larry up there—bungee jumping.

years, he stood at the brink of a life tragedy for which he was ill prepared. Diane had been Larry's shining light. She alone understood his rebellious nature. He had traveled across many lands to join her and now, suddenly, she was gone.

During his mysterious initiation into a greater mythic life, Larry had descended into a personal hell. This is a time of incredible (often-horrific) tests and adventures. "The hero moves in a landscape of curious fluid, ambiguous forms, where he must survive a succession of trials," writes Joseph Campbell. Here demons and monsters often lurk to devour the unwary. In this stage of the journey the hero is swallowed by the unknown; he experiences a death or death-like state and must employ extraordinary powers in order to return to the light of day. When successful, the hero of classic literature is often asked to return to the land of his birth. In Larry's story, he had the terrible duty of returning his sister's body home to New York.

It seemed at this time that the gods had turned their backs on Larry. The sunshine and light of his dreamland in California had turned into a nightmare. As he returned to the east coast with Diane's body, he must have felt that his young life was over. How could a just God allow such a thing to happen? How could the light of his life be snuffed out so suddenly by an uncaring creator? The questions began, and the enigma showed it's fanged teeth. Larry burned the conventions of polite society in the pit of his despair. The throbbing heartbeat of that old demon

contributed by BAMBI

Larry and friend from Area 51 at the Amboy Parade.

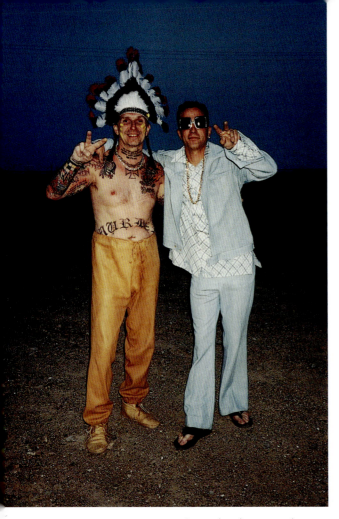

contributed by BAMBI

question mark was growing and beating loudly in his ears...why...why...why?

The Larry DeSmedt who returned to the home his father built was not the same laughing youth who sought adventure in California. A dark cloud surrounded him, and in his grief, drugs overtook him. Larry fell face-first into the seething monster, hoping it would devour him and end his pain. But, as so often happens in life, the easy way out turns out to not be so easy. Larry floundered in a sea of regrets and angst, turning away from his bright hopes and dreams. If God had turned his back on Larry by doing nothing to save his sister Diane, then Larry would turn his back on God—the gloves were off.

In turning away from the traditional Christian concept of a supreme deity, Larry found a new, lesser god in the drugs that brought sweet oblivion. This drug monster expected to be fed constantly and Larry found himself robbing local stores. The problem was that he was good at it. Local law enforcement knew what Larry was up to, but could never catch him.

"Apparently, Larry was a master of thievery in our local community," his sister Tina says. "The cops couldn't capture him and he was always stealing stuff. So they created a sting to capture him." The sting took the form of having a police informant working on the inside of Larry's criminal activities. One year after the death of his sister Diane, Larry robbed a bank. He had no idea that one of his accomplices had

Two things in life that make a big spark!

informed the police and when Larry waltzed out of the bank with a shotgun in one hand and a bag of cash in the other, the police were waiting for him.

Two of the cops opened fire on Larry and one managed to hit him. The bullet furrowed Larry's brow and the one-sided gunfight was suddenly over. Local newspaper pictures show the shotgun and bag of cash on the sidewalk in front of the bank. Another picture shows a grinning Larry in handcuffs, blood still seeping from his forehead. In typical Larry fashion, he was smiling as if he were playing cops and robbers as a kid and had been caught fair and square. "You got me!"

Larry's mother heard the news from a neighbor who asked if she had seen the daily paper. Her first reaction was, "What has my son done now?" Larry was just 23 years old at the time and went to prison for three years, spending most of his time in famous Sing Sing.

To truly know Larry, you have to understand that he rolled with life's punches. In typical Larry fashion, he was about to turn a bad thing into something very good. He would turn his time in prison into a holiday or vacation, using the time for contemplation and deeper learning, as a monk might use a monastery.

Inmate number 64442, as Larry was called, was about to enter the next great phase of the hero's journey. Larry was about to experience a psychological and spiritual death of old patterns and a rebirth as a new being, for what else is a prison but a tomb of sorts from which one

Posing for photos and signing autographs during BikeWeek in Daytona. Larry always had time for every fan.

photos by MICHAEL LICHTER

emerges a fresh, new being. What emerged in Larry's story is what ancient philosophers called the *anima mundi*, the soul of the world. Stepping into his greater self, Larry was about to discover a great truth. Walking in the footsteps of Percival or Odysseus, Larry came back to a life enhanced and empowered to prevail.

At this point in Larry's hero journey he entered a walk on the road of redemption, emerging from this dark night of the soul a new and more enlightened being.

The way I remember Larry most: riding with the wind in his hair and a smile on his face.

photos from INDIAN LARRY ARCHIVES

A familiar sight, Larry in his shop. The Rat Fink bike is on the lift, getting ready for the *Biker Build-Off*.

Pri-Zen

> "I got what I deserved. You can't do
> what I was doing.
> That's my advice, don't do what I did."
> INDIAN LARRY

BEFORE delving into the intricacies of the American prison system, it is important to understand the character of Larry DeSmedt. First of all, no one is born fully-fledged as Indian Larry, the icon and enigma, the biker shaman and coyote incarnate, the man with the tattoos on his neck. No, Larry became Indian Larry over a long period of time. Certainly his inquisitive nature was always there, as was his quirky sense of humor and unique sense of style. He was always a man of extremes. He once said, "I really like the extremes, y'know? It lets you know you're alive. When it's all nice and mellow, it's not for me." So, whether Larry was doing stunts on his motorcycle, lying on a bed of nails at the Coney Island Boardwalk, or jumping into sub-zero Atlantic Ocean with the Polar Bear Club, he became a person who constantly pushed his limits to the extreme.

It is important to note once again that a person only discovers his true nature through the perils of great adversity. Faced with a three-year prison term in New York's notorious Sing Sing prison, some men might just commit suicide rather than face their worst fears inside the Graybar

Larry's sister Tina says, **"Anything Larry set his mind to do, he did to an extreme.**

photos by TINA DeSMEDT-WELLS

Hotel, some might run away from the law to live constantly looking over their shoulder. Others excel in prison, learn to use the system, and become clerks for the facility's administrators. Many learn a trade, get a college degree, and return to the world a changed person. Larry was pragmatic when it came to doing his time. He realized that he had no choice but to go inside and deal with prison life, but Larry used his time in the same manner a monk uses his time in a monastery. He learned to meditate, he read a great deal, and he expanded his mind and consciousness. Prison became a school for Larry; he used his forced incarceration as a time for reflection, and in the process reinvented himself.

There are many classic myths that use this theme. Heroes such as Odysseus descended into Hades, the Greek underworld, to seek a prize or understanding and returned to the land of the living a new person. Such

In September of 1976, Larry was released from prison a new man. He got into body building and set out to become the best version of himself he could be.

Anything that Larry wanted to experience, he went above and beyond to experience it to the fullest."

resurrection myths occur in every land and time, from the resurrection of Osiris in ancient Egypt, to the Christ story, to the resurrection of Neo in *The Matrix* trilogy as a new program that governs cyber-reality. Humans have a great need for myth in their lives—our myths define us. As Dr. Jean Houston says in her great book, *The Hero and the Goddess*:

> *When we energetically and dramatically encounter this mythic realm and the beings that dwell there, we begin to understand that our individual lives—our personal stories—echo the events and truths of their lives and stories. We reflect these mythic beings and they reflect us. As such, we begin to live our lives on a larger scale and step into our true destiny.*

Larry did a lot of motor work for Psycho Cycles in the late 1990s.

Left to right; Keino, Paul Cox, Larry, and painter Robert Pradke during the filming of Larry's first *Biker Build-Off* episode.

Larry loved tinkering with older Harley motors and he was one of the best when it came to tuning them by ear.

photos from INDIAN LARRY ARCHIVES

This is essentially what happened with Larry. He learned to use a dire situation to his advantage. He stepped away from his small self, the everyday incarnation, and saw his world on a grander scale, a higher vision, a higher self.

Imagine being 23 years old and watching your life completely unravel around you. Your hopes and dreams have been dashed, your dearest loved one has been murdered, and you've destroyed whatever opportunity might have come your way by becoming a convicted felon. Your actions have disgraced your family. Now you must enter a completely separate reality where a person may be killed with a sharpened toothbrush for bumping into the wrong convict, for sitting at the wrong table during chow, or for talking to a person with a shade of skin other than your own.

The first thing that happens when you enter jail is that the prison guards give you a good delousing. This involves you stripping naked and running through showers while the guards spray insecticide on you. They then inspect ever orifice you've got to make sure you are not smuggling dope into the prison. You are then issued clothes that never fit and shoes that hurt your feet. Then you are placed in temporary housing while they figure out where you fit within the system, based on your crime.

There is a saying in prison that goes, "They can eat me, but they can't have me." This means that while the system can degrade a person, true freedom resides within. They can house your body, they can kill you, but they can not touch your spirit. They cannot cage your soul. The understanding of this was one step on Larry's road to enlightenment behind his pri-Zen.

Through the ages many have found enlightenment from within prison walls. Were it not for his long incarceration, Sir Thomas Malory

Psycho Cycles shop days.

would never have written the classic *Le Morte D'Arthur*. In Larry's case, he decided to construct a program to help pass his prison time and to better his mind, body, and spirit. This included a rigorous exercise program, constant study, and reflection. Larry had not finished high school, and so decided to get his GED diploma. He often wrote to his mother and asked for books. The first book he asked for was a dictionary, but soon, Larry was ready for the classics of literature as well as books on biophysics, philosophy, alternative religions, and quantum theory. He also enrolled in the prison's welding and mechanics courses. He got his GED and began taking college courses. During the three years of his incarceration, Larry became a Renaissance man.

photos from INDIAN LARRY ARCHIVES

According to his wife, Bambi, prison allowed Larry to hone his creative skills to a fine edge. "That's where he became a master mechanic. He always said that he was actually glad for his prison experience because that's where he honed all his best mechanical skills." Inmate No. 64442 was fast becoming a man with a new sense of drive and power. He was redefining himself on no less than the cellular level. Larry had found his entelechy and was stepping into a bigger world and cooking on more burners.

In the journey of the Native American shaman, there is always a defining moment in which the initiate takes on the mantle of the wise one. This is a part of any hero's journey. We see that the initiate goes through a ritual form of death and rebirth. In ancient Egypt, Mystery

Larry examines the work of his custom mentor, Ed "Big Daddy" Roth's famous chopper trike, *The Candy Wagon*, built in 1966.

contributed by BAMBI

Another famous Roth trike, The Mail Box was used as the heading image of the letter's column in "Big Daddy's" Choppers magazine in the 1960s.

EDDIE TROTTA

Thunder Cycle, Ft. Lauderdale, Florida

I first met Larry when they were filming *Motorcycle Mania I* in Sturgis with Jesse James. My first impression of him was that he was an old school, radical guy. Then we had a chance to hang out together at the *Easyriders* Bike Show Centerfold Tour. What impressed me about Larry was that he had time for everybody. He made people feel like he was close to them. That's why people loved him.

When I picture Larry in my mind I think of him standing up on the seat of his motorcycle, doing his little routine. The coolest thing was when he would lie down on his bike while rolling down the road, with his feet up on the handlebars—I could never do that. When I ride I think of Larry lying down on his bike, and I wonder how the hell he did that.

My favorite memory of Larry was from the second *Biker Build-Off* show he did. I was in Sturgis with him the day he cut the trophy up into pieces and threw it to the crowd. He was up against Billy Lane—stiff competition—but he knew that if he won, he would share the trophy with Billy. He always wanted to share everything with everybody.

Larry spent such a long time being virtually unknown, and then he made such a huge impact in such a short time. It was a short run of glory that will live forever now. I feel like 30 years from now Larry will still be a legend. He really influenced bike

Larry never minded taking photos with fans (Biketoberfest 2003), especially if they happened to be pretty girls.

School initiates actually entered a tomb and went through a near death experience in order to receive a visionary experience of their own death. This also happens with the shaman. Often, this vision is nothing less than vivid images of the destruction of the body. The shaman will see his body torn apart by animals or demons and then reconstructed and born in light as a new being. For Larry, prison offered this death and rebirth into a new form.

Rather than fall into the maya of destructive temporal games played by unintelligent inmates who could not see past their lower chakras, Larry went within to uncover a greater vision of himself. Rather than waste his time, he used it to call forth the wizard within and stepped forth from prison on a higher plane than the one on which he entered. It was during his prison time that Larry began to see the great truths. He embraced the concept that *now* is all that matters. The instant in which

building today by bringing back the old school bobber hot and heavy. He kept true to his roots and now there are hundreds of guys out there copying him. I really admired him because he was never too cool for anybody. He was available to all.

Looking back, we did a lot of bike shows together and we were like the old guys at the shows, from the same era. I would have liked to have spent more time with him. If there was one part of his life I wish I could have been present for, I would have liked to have been there the day he robbed that bank!

—*Eddie Trotta*

you find yourself at any given moment is the only eternity you have. Many convicts spend all their time lamenting on the past or hoping for a better future, thus completely missing the present. Larry learned that every present moment is a miracle and a gift. He began to live in the now in a very real way, discovering that when you make each now the best it can be, you automatically insure yourself great memories of the past as well as set yourself up for a positive future.

In September of 1976, Larry was released a new man. He went back home to upstate New York and continued the program he had designed for himself in prison. He continued to read and expand his consciousness and he also got into working out to stretch the limits of his physical self. Larry was on parole and stayed drug free and sober while becoming a body builder. At that time in his life he was the best version of himself

Paul Cox, Larry, and Bobby Seeger, the three amigos. photo from INDIAN LARRY ARCHIVES

Some lucky ladies even got a smooch.

photo by MICHAEL LICHTER

he could imagine. His sister Tina says, "Anything he set his mind to do, he did to an extreme. Anything that Larry wanted to experience, he went above and beyond it to gain the fullest experience."

This personal standard of excellence had nothing to do with keeping up with the Joneses or to prove anything to anyone. As his wife Bambi says, "It was never like he was doing it to go further than anyone else, or to purposely challenge an accepted boundary—it was just how he liked it. Larry liked it as hard and as fast and as cold or as extreme as it got."

On this hero's journey Larry had reached the discovery of the larger story, seeing his own life as part of a great life. As such, everyone Larry met became participants in the unfolding myth. He had also come through the initiation into the depths. He learned that initiations come in many forms and many of these are painful to complete. Now the question was, what would he do with this new life? The mystery of life was calling and the question mark still whispered in his ear.

The Biker Lifestyle

"The motorcycle represented life to him.
It's not just a technique or style; it's a philosophy."
PAUL COX

IN prison they hammer into you that you will never amount to anything, that you'll never succeed, and that you will be back. All the guards say it and you hear a million stories from other inmates about their hard luck and how difficult it is to make it through parole. To many in the system it seems that the parole officer's job is to make sure you end up back in prison—so the big money-making prison system can continue to be one of the biggest employers in America.

Larry stayed with his program, worked out, kept his eye on the goal, and managed to finish his time on parole without going back to the pen. He kept drawing and designing custom motorcycles, hoping for the day that he would build his own bikes. The idea of building choppers for a living was one of his great dreams, and once off parole, Larry moved to Manhattan and began working for various custom bike shops. He had learned many skills in prison, had honed his design talents, and was ready to create.

You can see why people thought Larry was a bad-ass at first glance. In this shot he looks like the person your mother warned you about. photo by MICHAEL LICHTER

Paul Cox and Larry relax by the water with friends (left to right) Chica, Big Chris, and Johnny Chop. photo by MICHAEL LICHTER

Design-wise, Larry liked to see all the parts of the motorcycle exposed. He liked to see all the gizmos, the clockworks of the bike. The art was in the function. "I like all the nuts and bolts and fittings, the linkages and the mechanicalness of it. I like to see all the mechanicalness," Larry said. He likened this to opening the back of a pocket watch and seeing all the internal components exposed and ticking away.

To Larry, a custom bike had to start with a raw, rigid frame (a chassis with no suspension); Larry preferred to work with the old-school frames built by Paughco, a company that has built bobber and chopper frames for over 35 years. Larry dug older Harley-Davidson motors such as the Panhead, which many purists consider to be the best looking motor that H-D ever built. And the motors were not mega-sized cubic inch monsters; Larry chose everyday functionality over massive horsepower. His bikes featured motors that were usually under 100 cubic inches and kick start only. He subscribed to the old saying: "If you can't kick start your bike, you have no right to be riding it." Larry's bikes were savage and maneuverable little road warriors that were well suited for blasting down the pot-holed streets of New York City.

During the 1980s Larry rode around Manhattan on a chopped Indian, and that's how he became known as Indian Larry. He became part of the New York art scene. Larry's wife Bambi says, "In the 1980s he hung out with Robert Maplethorpe and Andy Warhol, and they actually searched him out. They found him so fascinating that everyone wanted to be around him." Maplethorpe took lots of black-and-white photos of Larry and was one of the first artists to see Larry's mythic quality conveyed before his cameras. There's no doubt that the school of hard knocks had had its way with Larry. Some of the scars were visible, but Maplethorpe and Warhol were also no doubt fascinated with the

With Johnny Chop, who's riding a Billy Lane bike, Chica, and crew during Daytona BikeWeek. photo by MICHAEL LICHTER

Even while gassing up Rat Fink for a ride, fans came out of the woodwork to get Larry's autograph.

scars that didn't necessarily show on the outside, yet were captured on film. Here was a man who was bigger than life, who was "about something."

At the time Larry was also collecting tattoos that added to the enigma he carried around on his skin. Bambi remembers, "People would see Larry and literally cross the street because he looked so hardcore. People wouldn't sit next to him on the subway. But naturally, once you got to talking to him, you realized what a great sense of humor he had and what a great guy he was. You instantly had a friend for life."

Before the two bike builders had ever met, Billy Lane remembers seeing a picture of Larry and thought that he was a bad ass. "I just thought, this guy is gonna be trouble," Billy laughs. "But then I met him and he was just like this really genuine nice guy."

Larry was living his dream, building bikes in both New Jersey and in Manhattan, and living life on the edge. He was involved in the New York art scene, the performance art scene, the bike scene, and, unfortunately, he got back into the drug scene. His sister Tina remembers, "Once he went back and lived in the city, he got back into heroin and a whole other life that we [Larry's family] really don't know all that much about."

Indian Larry's bike building partner, Paul Cox, remembers watching Larry go through an internal roller coaster of ups and downs all the time.

photos by MICHAEL LICHTER

Billy Lane, executive producer of the *Biker Build-Off* series Hugh King, and Larry at party night in Sturgis. Billy's not mad, just hamming it up.

Party night at The Full Throttle Saloon. Larry hanging with Nicky "Boots" Fredella.

photos by MICHAEL LICHTER

"When it came to drugs, he was never totally clean until the last eight years of his life. He would quit drinking and doing drugs for awhile and be in top form. Then he would go through periods of time where he didn't think he deserved fame or whatever, and would sabotage himself by doing drugs," Paul says. "Larry would attack himself internally and head down a self-destructive spiral." Paul said that he and the guys who worked with Larry would see this look in his eyes and would know he was having a hard time. Then he would get help, get squared away, and he'd be right back on top again. "Larry would often get a shot at something, like a bike feature in a magazine, then blow it by doing drugs, but then he'd get clean and get right back on top again. He had the depth and knowledge to get back on top." Larry's ongoing battle with himself continued until the late 1990s. "It was like dealing with two different people," Paul remembers, "and they were always battling each other. But when Larry was on top, he gave everything two hundred percent. He was unstoppable."

There is a deeper meaning to the "becoming" of the persona known as Indian Larry. Larry's life echoed the initiations of the ancient Greek mystery cults. The rites of these mysteries provided journeys of anguish, grief, loss, redemption, and knowledge. Certainly Larry DeSmedt returned from his prison experience a wiser man in many ways and employed all that he learned in creating the man who became Indian Larry.

On Saturday, August 2, 2003, Larry and Billy Lane held a Sturgis Kick-Off Party at The Full Throttle Saloon as part of their *Biker Build-Off* competition. Doing burnouts 'til the tires popped was the order of the day.

Road Viking Paul Cox tears up the asphalt near Bear Butte, South Dakota. Paul is truly a David Mann painting come to life.

photo by MICHAEL LICHTER

Larry was a deep thinker. While a lighthearted jokester on the outside, he was capable of great insights and deep knowledge. He laughed about this aspect of himself. In fact, years later, after attaining much success and fame partially thanks to The Discovery Channel's motorcycle-related programs, Larry was asked what was going on inside his head. In typical Indian Larry fashion, he laughed and said, "Yeah, you don't want to go too deep inside there, it's very dangerous inside there, you'll get hurt."

But the fact of the matter was that Larry had learned how to take his great gifts and turn them into good box office. He was a showman and promoter who understood the value of publicity. He knew that his look and persona as Indian Larry could be bankable. He also knew that he was destined for greater things.

Unfortunately, like many of today's media stars, Larry was also his own worst enemy. Drinking and drugs continued to take their toll on him until he quit completely and became clean and sober in the late 1990s.

Larry worked at many different motorcycle shops during the 1980s and early 1990s. After prison, he began working for New Jersey shops including Crazy Horse and Whip's. This led to his first exposure in *Iron Horse*, a magazine dedicated to old school choppers and bobbers. Larry built bikes and motors out of his apartment on 8th Street, and between jobs he worked out of other people's bike shops in New York, places like Steinway's in Queens, American Dream Machine, and D.I.L.L.I.G.A.F.'s.

In 1988, artist Paul Cox came to New York from Richmond, Virginia. The talented artist got a job doing commercial art illustrations in Soho and also put on fine art shows in the area. Paul was into motorcycles and would work on them on the side, just for the love of it.

How would you like to be a fly on the wall, listening in on this conversation? Are they talking bike building or deep philosophy? My bet is that the subject of conversation is women!

Billy Lane and Larry riding together in Sturgis, 2003.

"After a couple of years I got sick of the commercial art scene and got more into my arts and crafts roots," Paul says. "I began doing hand-tooled leather motorcycle seats." Today, Paul is known all over the world for his incredible hand made saddles.

"I first met Indian Larry in 1990. I had heard of him before that but we met at a British bike shop called 6th Street Specials. Larry was building motors out of their place. Not long after that, we started working on bikes together at a place called Psycho Cycles on Avenue C in downtown Manhattan. I started doing leatherwork every night while Larry built bikes. Every night it was six-packs and Slim Jim's for dinner while we worked on bikes," Paul says with a smile. "Those were the days. We'd stay up working until two o'clock every morning. Staying late, no pressure, no worries."

Paul recalled that even in the early days of his association with Indian Larry, when he was on and off the wagon from time to time, it was a great ride. "I think of it as just a long journey, not as any specific special stories," Paul says. "It was an experience of extremes, both good and bad, but there were no in-betweens. Larry was a man of such extremes that every moment was an experience."

photos by MICHAEL LICHTER

Living in the now, signing autographs, shaking hands, kissing girls. Larry was a man of the people and they loved him for it.

photos by MICHAEL LICHTER

GREASE MONKEY

This is the bike that really put Larry on the map and defined the Indian Larry style of custom motorcycle. Besides being Larry's personal ride, *Grease Monkey* was also his first bike that was featured in *Easyriders* magazine (issue No. 303, September 1998). The article began, "Behold the chopper—it is form and function, pure unfettered brawn, yet torrid and sexual." The bike was called, "a statement in art, a living sculpture which screams of passionate rebellion." *Grease Monkey* is all that. The bike won the Editor's Choice Award that year at the prestigious *Easyriders* Invitational Bike Show in Columbus, Ohio, and was photographed by Michael Lichter. It was also the first bike of Larry's that Michael shot.

MOTOR: The Panhead motor in *Grease Monkey* was made from many parts from various years and had been pumped up to 1500cc. **PAINT:** The molding was by Larry with custom paint by Cassato Airbrush. **SEAT:** This was America's first look at a Paul Cox seat in *Easyriders* magazine.

photos by MICHAEL LICHTER

DADDY-O

Larry loved Ed "Big Daddy" Roth, and this bike was a tribute to his childhood hero. This is also the first bike Larry built for The Discovery Channel's *Biker Build-Off* TV series. From the mind-blowing hand-twisted Springer front end and signature Indian Larry Mustang-style gas tank, to the wild paint and question mark sissy bar, this scoot was Larry all the way. Master bike builder Paul Yaffe from Phoenix, Arizona, competed against Larry in the Build-Off before a live crowd during the Laconia Rally in 2003. The New Hampshire bike enthusiasts voted for their favorite bike and Larry won. *Daddy-O* was featured in the December 2004 issue of *Easyriders*.

FABRICATION: Larry touched every part on this bike with his creative hand. Check out the scallops cut into the exhaust. Even the gear shifter is a work of art. Notice how the bar is twisted this way and that. **PAINT:** Robert Pradke's wild paint is a tribute to Ed Roth, the father of Rat Fink and founder of *Choppers* magazine.

photos by MICHAEL LICHTER

photos by MICHAEL LICHTER

BERSERKER

A custom motorcycle should be as individual as its owner. A chopper makes a statement about who you are, and nowhere is this more true than with Paul Cox's personal ride, *Berserker*. Named after the legendary Viking warriors, this killer rigid Panhead is Paul's every day scooter and he rides the hell out of it. The details on *Berserker* are far too many to list here but the hand-built, girder-style front end and leather armor–inspired gas tank and rear fender let you know this pavement pounder could only belong to Paul.

FABRICATION: The oil travels through this maze of hand-curved hard lines. The rear fender struts were designed and cut by Paul to go with the Viking theme. Even the gas cap has attitude.

photos by MICHAEL LICHTER

MR. TIKI's SHOP DROPPINGS

Built with Bambi in mind, *Mr. Tiki's Shop Droppings* is a nod to the kitschy kind of Hawaiian décor you might find at Trader Vic's. Larry made the frame look just like bamboo and the Paul Cox seat looks like a basket weave usually reserved for palm fronds. *Mr. Tiki's Shop Droppings* traveled around the country in 2004 as part of the *Easyriders* Centerfold Tour and was the hit of over a dozen *Easyriders* Bike Shows. Larry called this Bambi's bike and you can imagine the tall, blonde mermaid astride it. All it needs is a bubble machine.

LEATHER: *Mr. Tiki's Shop Droppings'* seat by Paul Cox is reminiscent of a Polynesian basket made from palm fronds. **PAINT:** The bike's frame looks just like it was made from real bamboo. Robert Pradke's custom paint sells the illusion. Larry was a big fan of custom pinstriper Von Dutch. Here we see the kind of tiki face pinstriping that the master made famous back in the 1960s.

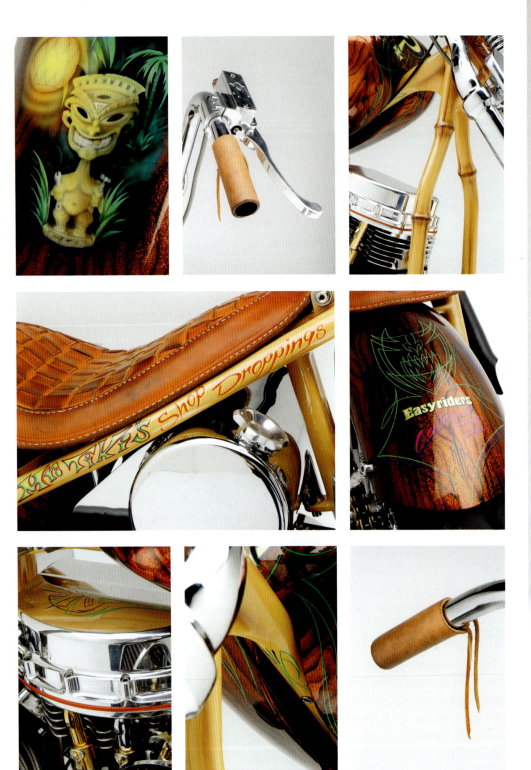

photos by MICHAEL LICHTER

photos by MICHAEL LICHTER

WILD CHILD

Created for the second *Biker Build-Off* episode in which Larry competed, *Wild Child* went up against a chopper built by Billy Lane of Choppers Inc. The vote was held during the Sturgis Rally in 2003 and when Larry won the popular vote his first thought was to cut the trophy down the middle and share it with Billy. But Billy and Larry decided to cut the trophy in a bunch of pieces, autographing each one and throwing the pieces out to the audience. *Wild Child* is truly unique in that it has a Shovelhead front cylinder and a Panhead rear.

ENGINE: The one-off motor also ran two carburetors, a real pain in the ass to tune.
LEATHER: Another great hand-tooled leather seat by Paul Cox shows a cartoony characterization of Larry. **CONCEPT:** The open belt drive is the perfect place to paint the name of this bike. Larry was the ultimate wild child.

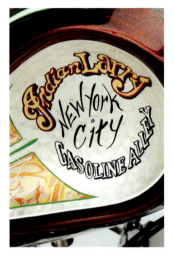

photos by MICHAEL LICHTER

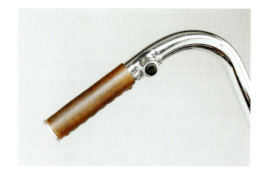

photos by MICHAEL LICHTER

CHAIN OF MYSTERY

Larry pulled out all the stops for his third and last *Biker Build-Off* chopper. This time he was pitted against old-school master Mondo Porras of Denver's Choppers in Henderson, Nevada. The Indian Larry team started by welding together heavy chain to make the frame. No one thought the chain frame would hold together but it came through, in spades. Amazingly detailed engraving on the bike by C. J. Allen and intricate paint by Robert Pradke blew everyone's mind. Larry died on the very day that the votes were being cast at the Liquid Steel Motorcycle Show in Concord, North Carolina.

DETAIL: Check out C. J. Allen's engraving on the brass knuckles kick-start pedal. Every part of *Chain of Mystery* was detailed to the max. Here is an engraved Panhead rocker box cover.

LEATHER: Another great Paul Cox seat, this time showing the wild cartoon of Indian Larry used in a T-shirt design.

photo by MICHAEL LICHTER

ZARATHUSTRA'S REVENGE

When S&S Cycle came out with their new reproduction Shovelhead engines, several top bike builders were asked to create unique rides to showcase the new motor. Indian Larry Legacy stepped up to the plate with this nasty little rigid with drag bike overtones. The S&S bike is pure Indian Larry, from the twisted downtube of the frame, to the trick engine detailing, to the Paul Cox–hand tooled leather seat.

PAINT: The custom paint on the gas tank by Robert Pradke was the second bike that incorporated angel wings into Larry's question mark logo. The winged logo first appeared on *Love Zombie*'s seat.
LEATHER: The Paul Cox leather seat shows the Super "B" carburetor schematic. **CONCEPT:** In the great mystery tradition of Indian Larry, the bike's name, *Zarathustra's Revenge*, is another enigma. You see, the last thing the ancient creator of Zoroastrianism, which preached "cause and effect" in the universe, would seek is revenge.

photos by MICHAEL LICHTER

BROOKLYN BEATNIK

This bike was built for the *Easyriders* Centerfold Tour in 2005 by Indian Larry Legacy and traveled to bike shows all over the country. It truly shows an amazing amount of one-off fabrication and innovative designs. Larry always talked about liking to see "the mechanical-ness" of a motorcycle. He loved to explore a bike the way you would the inner workings of a pocket watch. Paul and Keino certainly went all out to show us every fascinating nut and bolt on this chop. The work on the twisted Springer front end alone makes the *Brooklyn Beatnik* a true work of art.

FABRICATION: Imagine heating up the metal white hot and twisting it just so to create this amazing front end. **CONCEPT:** Perhaps the name of this scoot is a tip of the hat to Ed Roth and kustom kulture of the 1960s. One of Roth's most famous custom cars was called *Beatnik Bandit*.

DETAIL: Larry would be mighty proud of Paul and Keino. Just look at the details of this amazing ride. There's no doubt Larry would have spent hours looking at every wild detail and "the mechanical-ness" of it all.

photos by MICHAEL LICHTER

TEMPTING FATE

Each year, photographer Michael Lichter holds a gallery show at The Journey Museum in Rapid City, South Dakota, during the Sturgis Motorcycle Rally in August. In 2005 he asked a dozen or so top builders to create special custom bikes to go with the year's theme, Speed Demons. For their entry, Indian Larry Legacy built a strictly business road scorcher made to blast down the mean streets of New York City. *Tempting Fate* is a bike that Larry would have loved to tear around on.

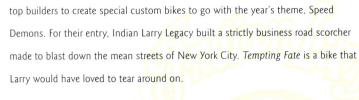

CONCEPT: The name says it all. If the devil is in the details, this is one hellacious ride. **FABRICATION:** Hand-made pipes above the clutch basket, etched to make sure you know who built it.

photos by MICHAEL LICHTER

Biker, artist, mystic, shaman, and bigger than life—Indian Larry. contributed by BAMBI

To Hell and Back

"The eye by which I see God,
is the same eye by which God sees me."
MEISTER ECKHART

MANY can relate to the years of Indian Larry's life in which he bounced back and forth between brilliance and lunacy. After all, madness and genius are closely related. There were times when Larry felt that he was almost there, treading close to magnificence, but there was a part of him that felt he did not deserve success and fame.

Larry built bikes in the mid-1990s that he felt should be on the cover of *Easyriders*. Being on the cover of America's biggest and best biker magazine was a huge deal for him. "What do ya think?" he asked. "Will this one make the cover?" His face was like a child's, filled with hope. I had the unhappy duty of informing him that the bike did not make the cover. His lean streetfighter bikes were not the style back then and *Easyriders*' readers wanted to see Easter egg–colored billet barges. Larry was crestfallen. Suddenly, nothing was good enough; not the bike and not himself. He was almost there, so close that he could taste it, and the frustration of being close but no cigar was one of the reasons he

At the Coney Island Tattoo and Motorcycle Show that Larry hosted every year with friend Eak the Geek. photo by ROBERT DOMINGO

would become depressed. During his low times Larry dropped back into a drugged stupor, as if to punish himself.

It was very frustrating for Larry to be a passionate artist who poured his heart into his motorized masterpieces and got little praise, but Larry was ahead of his time. By the late 1990s, when he was straight and focused, his style of mechanical marvels became very popular and he eventually had custom bikes in *Easyriders* and its sister publication *V-Twin*. But first, Larry had to get through the late 1980s and early 1990s—a time often remembered as Larry's time in the University of Hell. A tattoo on Larry's arm brands the dates of his release from this horrid place of learning. "Yeah, the University of Hell 1991 and 1994," Larry laughed. "I had to go through it twice—a lot of hard work to finally get to that point."

And so Larry entered that phase of the hero's journey in which the figure sunk into the deeper process through which he will emerge victorious. This time is traditionally fraught with peril of many kinds and the hero usually finds that he is cast upon the oceans of sorrow and delight with equal abandon. Indian Larry eventually emerged as a new being and as such, this new avatar was tested time and time again. All heroes must undergo the growth and trauma required for a new birth into the world. They act as savior for us all by way of example.

Joseph Campbell reminds us that at any point along the path of our journey we may experience several stations and conditions of the quest at the same time. At this point in Indian

contributed by BAMBI

Larry with "Ms. Biker Slut" at the annual Indian Larry party at Coney Island.

Larry on a bed of nails with a heavy weight applied.

A few words with the Ice Cream Man from Hell.

photos from INDIAN LARRY ARCHIVES

Larry's life he encountered a series of initiations into his own depths. During these life experiences he discovered the many forms of initiation through pain and suffering so that he might rise above and move to a new stage of being.

In all times and places the rites of the ancient mysteries provided powerful initiations through the doorways of anguish and loss, through the portals of redemption and knowledge, and finally, metaphorically, the hero comes to stand in ecstatic union with a god or goddess. The hero often dies to one form of life only to be reborn to a new one. This may happen over and over again on the journey, as happened with Larry.

Indian Larry's deep knowing of the mysteries led to his acquiring the question mark as his life's logo. "Roll with the mystery," Larry said. He had a lot to roll with. We live in a time when entire systems are in transition, a time in which the very concept of reality is being rewritten. As Dr. Jean Houston says in her book *Jump Time*, "We find ourselves

Laying on a bed of nails is hard enough, but having Larry stand on you at the same time has gotta hurt!

The members of the Polar Bear Club enjoy taking a dip in freezing waters.

at present in the midst of the most massive shift of perspective humankind has ever known." It is no wonder that Larry had difficulty standing amid the thrashing winds of change.

Heroes take on the very fabric of the times in which they live. This is true of Indian Larry and is the key to why people find him so fascinating. Yes, he was an enigma; there was mystery in the man with the tattoos on his neck. But there was also the very human aspect of Larry that everyone could relate to. Here was a shaman who was right for the times, a wizard of the people.

contributed by BAMBI

American life underwent enormous change during Larry's life. The maps that guided him in his youth no longer fit the territories he found himself in as a man. Everything was in transition, becoming something else entirely—but what? Think about human history. For thousands of

PAUL YAFFE
PYO, Phoenix, Arizona

The first time I met Larry face-to-face was when I walked into his shop, Gasoline Alley, in Brooklyn. I was there as part of The Discovery Channel's *Biker Build-Off* episode where I was pitted against Larry. I had seen Larry on TV with Jesse James but when I walked into his shop to meet him I had no prior contact with him and was a little intimidated. I was alone and I thought he was going to be tough, tattooed, and badass with a gang of tough-looking guys. As it turned out he was very gracious. The bike I built for the show had arrived at his place the day before so

Larry was a proud member of the Polar Bear Club in Coney Island.

he and his crew had a chance to check it out. I feel that the bike gained me some respect points before I got there. I kind of expected Larry's bike to be an old school bobber but I was totally blown away with its Rat Fink look. The quality of the workmanship just knocked my socks off. I think I was overly confident about my chances at winning until I saw his bike.

The thing about Larry was that he was without ego. He seemed comfortable with himself and his art. He didn't care what anybody else thought of the bikes he built; he did it for the art. He always enjoyed the spotlight and the attention he got. And he always had time for people; he'd give anybody respect and listen to what they had to say. Larry had a way of making people have fun—he knew how to pump up an audience. At the bike rallys he would sit in this cool carved throne chair with question marks on it and hold court. He looked like something out of Batman and The Joker, but clad in sweatpants, a white wife-beater, and flip-flops. People would climb up into his lap as if he were Santa Claus. I think people loved him and they wanted to be around him because he had a way of making people feel better about themselves—I know he made me feel that way.

When we were in Laconia for the *Build-Off* show, he and I got to ride all day, a very long day, through rain and sunshine—he smiled all day. That's how I picture Larry, riding and smiling. He always had a huge smile on his face and a great laugh. What impressed me most about Larry was that he was true to himself. He was honest and stuck by his guns. He saw things a certain way and that was it. He didn't bend to fads or sell out for financial gain. He was Indian Larry, first and foremost.

Indian Larry loved extremes. He thought there was nothing that was more fun than stripping down and riding a bike in the icy snow.

years, the life that your forefathers lived did not change significantly. Your great grandparents probably lived and died within a few miles of where they were born. Their station in life changed little; the father's occupation was visited upon the son, and so on. But within the past 50 years our world has changed at an accelerated rate the likes of which the planet has never known. We are literally standing at the brink of an entirely new way of life, filled with energy, filled with the very stuff of creation, and we are all asking ourselves where we fit in this world that is still becoming. In every way you can think of, we as a species are being remade. And though we may not recognize it, some of us may, too, be taking the same heroic, mythical path Larry took.

For Larry DeSmedt, the time of his passing through and being remade was at hand in a way more terrible and compelling than anything he had so far experienced. Heroin proved to be a mighty temptress, one

photos by PAUL COX

I know that if Larry walked through the doors of my shop right now he'd have his arms open wide for a hug and call me brother. I'd stop whatever I was doing and show him around. Then we'd go off to a strip club or do something to cause some trouble. I always felt very fortunate to be with Larry and I miss him every day. People come up to me at bike shows and want to talk to me about him. I always tell people that we miss him. Without him, the road is different, the tours are different. He always brought huge life to any party. The man was just outrageous.

Larry influenced custom bike building today with his loyalty to the old school—he kept old school cool. His devotion and passion for old-world, build-it-yourself craftsmanship really helps us all remember our roots as bike builders and helps us remember what is really cool.

It seems it is getting harder and harder to make a living in this industry. So many custom bikes look the same. Larry's fortune was in satisfying himself with his craft. He was blessed because the creative part of bike building was his payday. Larry's work helps us all remember why we do what we do for a living. He was all about building bikes that you can ride the hell out of, instead of building bikes that are for show. He reminds me that there is only one way to do things.

The one thing that Larry said to me that I'll never forget is something that he said many times. We would be at a bike show or rally somewhere and someone would ask to take our picture. He would put his arm around me and smile, and then he would lean in close to my ear and say, "Isn't this cool?"

—*Paul Yaffe*

he was no match for. As the 1980s evolved into the 1990s, Larry found himself living in New York's seedy Bowery and encountering another dark night of the soul. "I was homeless, shirtless, penniless, showerless. I had nothing left," Larry said during an interview in front of The Discovery Channel cameras. He did whatever it took to feed the needle. It has often been said that true redemption only occurs after you hit absolute bottom. In November of 1991, Larry once again hit bottom—perhaps an even deeper bottom than the one that had landed him in prison. He was coming down hard, had cut himself with a broken bottle, and was staggering, wandering, and bleeding down the grim streets of regret. A cop car stopped and shown a bright searchlight in Larry's face. "Just shoot me," he dared the police. They took him to Bellevue Mental Hospital instead.

photo from INDIAN LARRY ARCHIVES

"When you get to the absolute bottom, there's nowhere to go but up or die," Larry said. "So . . . I'm not a big believer in suicide. No matter how bad it gets I figure it's not my job to kill myself."

It is interesting that in all native cultures, the medicine man or shaman must pass through a rite of initiation wherein he or she loses the mortal body and is reborn. This can be created through great ceremony including a scarification. It may occur as a dream walk through the outback to survive alone, or as some form of ritualistic battle, or many times, it may involve a sweat lodge and the use of hallucinatory drugs to open the portals of the worlds. Here, in an altered state, the initiate crosses between the worlds. He may receive a blessing or discover his totem animal and the powers associated with it, or many times, the shaman is symbolically torn apart by savage beasts. Once his former earth

The members of the Indian Larry Flying Circus at Coney Island.

Larry and Bambi at the Coney Island Mermaid Parade.

photo by LAURE LEBER

body is destroyed, he is reborn anew as a being of light. Thus the shaman steps forth back into the world of his tribe, a new an empowered being. He has become the man who walks in two worlds and a wizard of great power.

In Larry's life, the time had come to surrender to the thrashing demons. They tore him apart and allowed him to be rebuilt anew, in a greater vision of who he really was. His sister Tina reflected, "I think it was through Bellevue that he finally got connected to Alcoholics Anonymous and Narcotics Anonymous and really decided to stop the drug situation and turn his life into something of enduring value that he wasn't going to destroy anymore."

But that assessment is far easier identified and said than done. Larry found the long journey back up from the pit of despair to be an arduous trek. "I struggled on back up the ladder," Larry said. "It wasn't easy, like waving a wand. It was very, very difficult and I don't think I could do it again. It was too hard." Luckily, Larry was addicted to motorcycles and channeled his passion into a positive expression. The very bad boy image and thunderous murder cycles that had created him ultimately became his salvation.

That, and the love of a good woman.

How many guys get to marry a mermaid? Here Bambi is pushed around on a hand truck—it's hard to walk while wearing flippers! photo by NORMAN BLAKE

contributed by BAMBI

The Hero and the Goddess

"Larry was the opposite
of what you might think he'd be like.
He had a huge impact on people,
but didn't take himself so seriously."

BAMBI, *Larry's wife*

INDIAN Larry's journey had led him down the long road of recovery. The hero's journey often involves the hero passing through the world of unfamiliar yet strangely intimate forces. When he arrives at the heart of the mythological realm, he undergoes a supreme ordeal. In Indian Larry's case, the loss of his finger as a child only became part of his armor. The loss of his sister allowed her to become a magical calaid (helper) in his times of need. Even his time in prison was used to learn and grow from without and within.

For Larry, drugs represented the supreme spiritual ordeal to overcome. Here were the monsters of his soul, of his own making, the demons of self doubt. How many people have heard and answered many calls, discovered remarkable allies, crossed forbidden thresholds, been chewed up and spit out of the belly of the whale, entered rocky roads of

Just an all-American couple.

Larry riding with superstar Harrison Ford.

contributed by BAMBI

trials and wild adventures? Have we not all fought with monsters of our own or others' making, tried to right wrongs, or make the quality of life better for ourselves or someone we care about? Then congratulations, my friends, for you too are on this amazing journey.

Larry's self-proclaimed University of Hell involved nightmarish travels through the dark night of the soul. None but the most valiant survive this process for "here there be monsters" of the worst kind. Here Larry encountered his own monsters and did the very difficulty personal work necessary for his graduation from this demonic college of extreme hard knocks. As with all such heroes' journeys and great stories, Larry's particular one includes the reward for surviving the great ordeal. In such classic myths, the hero undergoes a sacred marriage, often to a true goddess. In Larry's case, he married a mythical character: the mermaid.

Archetypes incarnate, modern mystics, and madly in love.

Our shaman biker's future bride performed at Coney Island, where she was known as Bambi the Mermaid. "We met in 1996 or so," Bambi says. "I knew about Larry because we ran in the same world in the east village." Bambi was dating a biker named Lizard, at the time. Lizard followed Indian Larry's work through bike features in motorcycle magazines and had shown Bambi pictures of Larry and his bikes. "Larry was a mythic legend. I knew other girls who had dated him and had talked to them about what he was like. I thought he was the coolest, greatest thing ever.

"Whenever I would see Larry around at an art opening or whatever, he would flirt with me in a major way. I was flattered but intimidated by him, too. Then, one night Kate, my best friend at that time, called me and said that the man of my dreams was at the bar where she was working. She kept on about it and I ended up going over there. Well, there was Larry. Kate loved Larry too and told him that I was the woman of his dreams as well.

"Larry was still drinking at that time and he and I had a couple of drinks and ended up making out for five hours. He was playing Roy Orbison and Patsy Kline and all this romantic music on the juke box, and he actually started crying, saying, 'No one else will ever truly know my soul.' I remember thinking, 'I will. I could do that.' But I was still pretty intimidated by him. I remember thinking that I would probably have one wild night with Indian Larry and that would be it. I gave him my phone number and he called me the next day. We would talk on the phone occasionally, or see each other at art shows, steal a kiss here and there, but I always had a boyfriend at the time. Larry would call me and keep in touch from time to time.

contributed by BAMBI

Larry in mystic garb as part of the Amboy Parade.

Bambi calls this,
"The happiest day of my life."

Appropriately, the bride and groom said their vows at the Coney Island Sideshow with assorted friends and freaks in attendance.

contributed by BAMBI

"Then, one night I was with Kate when Larry showed up at the bar. He said that his best friend was having a bachelor party that Friday night and that he needed girls for the party. That meant he needed strippers. Well, I do an old fashioned burlesque theatrical striptease and Larry wanted Kate and me to come to his friend's party and do a routine. 'There's gotta be girls!' he said. Kate had had a few drinks and agreed to go with me to the bachelor party. Now, my burlesque striptease is very nostalgic and PG-rated, not exactly the kind of stripping you'd want at a bachelor party, but I didn't want to disappoint Larry.

"The night of the party came and Kate backed out on me. I wasn't about to let Larry down so I got another friend to come with me. She was very prudish but what are ya gonna do? We went over to Larry's apartment and met the groom to be: Paul Cox. There were all these biker guys that I had seen around New York sitting around in a semi circle, waiting for the strippers. It was a mortifying experience. I did my best to strip a little. Well, Paul is the most exemplary gentleman you would ever want to meet. Larry had me sit on Paul's lap and Paul just kept his hands clamped to the armrests of the chair he was in. Meanwhile, my prudish girlfriend didn't do *anything!* The pressure was all on me.

"Then Larry went to the refrigerator and came back with two cans of whipped cream. He applied whipped cream to my boobs and tried to get Paul to lick it off. But, ever the gentleman, Paul refused and Larry ended up licking it off himself. I told Larry that it was time for me to go and started getting dressed. He asked if he could walk me home. The thing is, the party was in his apartment, so he ended up kicking everybody out—'party's over, get out!'—so that he could walk me home.

On the way home he asked to see me the next night. Neither of us was seeing anybody at the time, so we started dating the next day and

What bigger-than-life wedding would be complete without a host of mermaids?

The happy couple on their wedding day, June 3, 2000.

were pretty much inseparable after that. The funny thing is that now Paul is like my brother, the apartment where it all started is where I still live, and even my landlord was at the bachelor party. That night turned out to be a moment of fate or destiny. I came into the fold as the stripper at Paul's bachelor party. It was so typical of Larry to whip something together at the last minute and have it be a smashing success."

Bambi and Larry began dating in 1997. "We went to Coney Island for our first date," Bambi remembers. "There was a Coney Island Tattoo and Motorcycle Convention that Larry was a part of. I remember that we rode on his bike, *Grease Monkey* (featured in *Easyriders* magazine No. 303, September 1998). I wore white leather pants and had a really hard time lifting my legs onto the passenger pegs, which were about one inch long. I had to grip really tight and he was not one to ride slow. My life flashed before my eyes a hundred times that night. You could say that I got pretty good at hanging on for dear life."

That first date went well for both Bambi and Larry. Looking back at their early days together Bambi remembers, "I was in awe of Larry. At first I thought he was gonna be a notch in my belt—I really didn't expect it to turn out to be something more." But Larry turned out to be a multifaceted and very endearing character.

Bambi says that most people would see Larry and expect him to be some sort of bad ass, but the opposite was true. "He was so affectionate and funny. We would go out together and he would hold my hand and

contributed by BAMBI

> The gods smiled down on Larry and Bambi. It was a picture perfect day.

never let go of it." She remembers dating rough biker-types who acted too cool to hold her hand or introduce her to their friends. Not so with Larry, "He was always proud to be seen with me and introduced me to everyone. I was intimidated by him at first, but he was so funny and I thought he was the coolest thing that ever walked the planet."

Bambi owns a lot of wild costumes and funny props. She remembers watching Larry dress up in silly masks and apparel and dance around like a modern day Loki (Norse god of mischief). "Larry was the opposite of what you might think he'd be like. He had a huge impact on people but he didn't take himself so seriously." As we all know from countless *Playboy* surveys of their cover girls, women are attracted to men who can make them laugh. Plus, as Bambi reminds us, women seemed to detect the mythic within Larry.

One of the reasons Indian Larry was a mythic character and had the ability to show so many complex facets of his personality has to do with a very old Mystery School practice. Larry had the ability to tap into his "inner crew," meaning he learned to utilize all the various masters that walk within each of us. If Larry wanted to access the part of himself that was a master chef for instance, he was able to go to that place within where his inner crew exist as real beings. He could then "download" whatever information he required in the timeless time that exists in this altered state, and use that information to create the perfect gourmet dish.

People who have this amazing human potential are called polyfrenic. They are literally able to access more of their own innate abilities and stay in touch with multiple facets of their being on all levels. Larry was cooking on more than one burner, for he was aware of his deeper, mythic levels of being. This ability was also very attractive to women, who could tell that there was a great deal going on with

photo by Laurie Leber

contributed by BAMBI

A man comfortable in his own skin, Larry knew how to have the maximum amount of fun wherever he went. This was taken on his honeymoon.

Larry below the surface. This, no doubt, added to the air of mystery that surrounded him.

Bambi and Larry began seeing quite a bit of each other and Bambi soon became the anchor that Larry needed in his life. They performed at Coney Island where Larry was known for doing famous sideshow stunts such as lying on a bed of very sharp nails. Mystic abilities like these show that Larry could consciously enter into altered states at will in order to perform amazing feats. Our hero had become the man who lives in two worlds, the physical and the spiritual. In Bambi, our hero found the Goddess he was seeking, the beloved of the soul.

Larry was 49 years old and had never married. In Bambi he discovered another artistic being who complimented his complex personality. He proposed to Bambi on her 31st birthday on an empty beach in the Bahamas. "It was just the two of us, just standing out there on the beach and it was sunset and really romantic," Bambi recalls. "And Larry said, 'Do you want to see your birthday present?' and I said okay, and he took off his shirt and had 'Bambi' tattooed over his heart in circus letters. I was pretty taken aback. I was speechless. And he said, 'You know, you only have one girl's name tattooed over your heart in a lifetime.' And I thought, oh, that's what that means!"

In all of this strange and wacky world, Indian Larry had found the perfect mate, someone to share a universe that was grander and more complex than all his dreams. They had a kitchy Coney Island wedding and got married at the sideshow. From pictures taken at their wedding reception it is easy to see that Bambi and Larry's hearts were bursting with happiness.

We have reached a very important place in our travels with Larry, for he has lived through the turmoil, the horror, and the madness of his

photo by GRACE MARTINI

hero's journey, to arrive at a place of triumph. In classic myths this is often represented as the hero's sexual union with the Goddess. Intrinsically, it is an expansion of consciousness and therewith of being (illumination, transfiguration, freedom). Our hero has returned home to love, to family, to new beginnings. It was at this point that the Indian Larry known to millions all over the world took his place on the center stage.

Larry and Bambi riding on *Grease Monkey*.

photo by NORMAN BLAKE

The Original Productions video crew shoots Larry for the first *Biker Build-Off* episode he was in against Paul Yaffe at New York's Sideshows by the Seashore Freak Show.

Media Magician

"The motorcycle is like a sacred object to me.
When I go out for a ride, I'm exactly in the moment.
It's like meditation; I'm in the flow."
INDIAN LARRY

INDIAN Larry had become a man of two worlds, effectively working in both the physical and spiritual realms, existing in both of them effortlessly. His polyfrenic abilities also allowed him to manipulate reality—to a certain degree. He was ready to focus on building motorcycles and create the Indian Larry brand. It is interesting to note that Larry was just beginning to gain the notoriety that he is known for today.

One of the ways that a custom motorcycle fabricator builds his reputation is to have his bikes showcased in motorcycle magazines. Larry had been featured in a few regional magazines and in *The Horse*. But his first big break was his debut in *Easyriders* magazine in the February 1998 issue (No. 296, pages 87 to 91). The story was titled, "Hardcore NYC Troubadors" and offered stunning black-and-white photos of Indian Larry and his trusty old rigid Shovelhead, along with his building and riding friends from Psycho Cycles. These included Paul Cox (who began

Larry with the *Hot Dog Rod* from The Discovery Channel's *Monster Garage* TV series.

working with Larry at Psycho Cycles in 1994) on a leather-clad, jockey shift Triumph, and other NYC Psycho Cycles partners Stag Von Heinz, Walt Segle, and Psycho Frank. The men were pictured in front of the Belly of the Beast tattoo joint—offering the best ink in town—and the Red Rock West Saloon.

The memorable thing about this article is that it was not about the bikes Larry built; rather it was focused on the difficulties of riding in New York City and how hard core a rider needed to be to blast through the mean streets. The article was more about building Larry's persona as an epic character. It was here that the world first saw Indian Larry sporting his infamous neck tattoo. Even this added to the mystery. What did it say and why would someone want to tattoo their neck? Hell, he *must* be hardcore!

When asked about the tattoo, Larry explained that it was his way of always reminding himself not to judge others. The neck tattoo is written as follows:

photos from INDIAN LARRY ARCHIVES

IN GOD WE TRUST

ƎNIM SI ƎƆNAƎGNƎV

ᗡЯOJ ƎHT HTƎYAS

NO FEAR

The reversed Bible verse reminded Larry that, "Vengeance is mine, sayeth the Lord." It was a constant reminder to Larry that revenge was not his job. For everyone who knew Larry closely, the caption to the picture of him and his bike in *Easyriders* must have evoked a lot of laughter. "Indian Larry—the world's angriest man." Though Larry

Being interviewed during the annual Bike Show at the Javitz Center in New York.

The famous neck tattoo. Larry once said that it was his way of reminding himself that he is not here to judge.

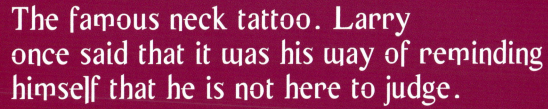

Holding court at the Broken Spoke during the 2004 Laconia Rally in New Hampshire. Larry's *Biker Build-Off* winning *Daddy-O* is in the background.

photo by MICHAEL LICHTER

Larry, hanging at Billy Lane's Choppers Inc. with Nicky "Boots" Fredella.

certainly looked foreboding in the picture, he was best known for his kindness to others and for his honesty and integrity in business and in life.

Larry's next big break came with his first custom bike feature shown in an International magazine. *Easyriders* is translated into many languages and sold all over the world with a monthly readership of over 3 million motorcycle lovers. It has been the "biker's Bible" for over 35 years and to Larry, a bike feature in *Easyriders* meant that he had arrived in the upper echelon of motorcycle culture. He got that opportunity in the September 1998 issue with a full-color feature on his custom chopper that he called *Grease Monkey* (No. 303, pages 19 to 23). That particular issue was my second one as editor-in-chief and I was proud to show Larry's lean and mean scooter. *Grease Monkey* had won the prestigious Editor's Choice Award at our *Easyriders* Invitational Bike Show (the Academy Awards of bike shows) in Columbus, Ohio. The bike was shot by, in my opinion, the best motorcycle photographer in the world, Michael Lichter. This was a huge honor for Larry. He was on the map. Quoting the article by English Don (later of *The Horse* magazine), "This could be the finest hardcore chopper ever created. Indian Larry is the medicine man." And so, from John Q. Public's perspective, the Indian Larry legend began.

Through his motorcycle stunt work and Coney Island side show performances, Larry had developed a mythic character for himself. He was the tattooed man and the sword-swallower; he was the Indian shaman and custom motorcycle artist; he was the enigma, the question mark; he was . . . a very long way from his childhood in upstate New York and the DeSmedt family.

But for all those who worked closely with Larry and spent a great deal of time with him, he was defined by his strong, personal integrity

photos by MICHAEL LICHTER

Billy Lane and Larry check out Jesse Jurrens' latest ride.

and jovial nature. Larry's business partner in his Indian Larry clothing line is a lovable character in his own right named Bobby Seeger. Bobby's talented wife Elisa has been running the office at the bike shop since 2003. She briefly met Larry and Bambi at their wild Coney Island wedding in 2001 and was amazed at how different Larry and Bambi were from conventional society. "Bambi wore a Mermaid wedding dress, how cool is that?" Elisa says.

When the time came to have the first meeting with Larry about working at the shop as his new business manager, Elisa remembers being a little intimidated. "I came to the shop in Brooklyn at night. There was graffiti all over the brick walls and it was dark. I walked into the shop and there were all these motorcycles and there was Larry with all his tattoos," Elisa says. "But he put me at ease right away. He was so warm and down to earth. I instantly believed in him and wanted to help him with his vision."

contributed by BAMBI

DAVE PEREWITZ

Cycle Fabrications, Bridgewater, Mass.

The one word that best sums up Indian Larry is *showman*. I first met him while taping Larry's first *Biker Build-Off* show for The Discovery Channel. Larry was up against Paul Yaffe and the producers of the show asked me to ride along with them from New York City to Laconia, New Hampshire. We got there during the Laconia Bike Week, and it was crazy.

I have to admit that I had never heard of Indian Larry before The Discovery Channel's *Motorcycle Mania* show with Jesse James. I remember pulling into Laconia and there was Larry. He was very cordial and glad to meet me and we became friends fast. The thing about Larry was that he was a true character. He was a character in the motorcycle industry.

One story that stands out in my mind was the time we were riding along on the back roads of New Hampshire, out in the middle of nowhere. We pulled over for a moment because the Discovery cameras were going to film us riding, when all of a sudden this carload of teenagers pull up and get out of their car. They yelled out, "It's Indian Larry!" I mean, it was as if these kids just saw Elvis. They were really starstruck. All of us were laughing except Larry. He took their devotion very seriously. He shook their hands and gave them autographs, and spent some time with them. Larry was like that with everyone, always extremely gracious.

Larry with his beloved "kids," Willow and Mr. Velvet Underpants.

Elisa recalls two fond memories of Larry that show his compassion and thoughtfulness for others and integrity in life. "We were going to Columbus, Ohio, for the *Easyriders* Invitational Bike Show," Elisa explains. "Bobby was driving the truck and trailer with all the bikes and clothing in it. The Columbus Show takes place each year on Valentine's Day and over that weekend in February. I met Larry at the airport and flew with him to the bike show. Larry pulled out a Valentine's card and gave it to me. I was speechless! I guess Bambi had wanted to know why Larry had bought two cards and he told her, 'I have to get one for Elisa, because, you know, she and Bobby will be apart on Valentine's Day.' How sweet is that? I still have that card from Larry."

Then, at another bike show in Somerset, New Jersey, Elisa was strolling around the show and stopped at a leather booth. "They had all these leather bracelets with different names etched into them and there was one that said 'Bambi.' It had pink hearts all over it and I bought it

photo by MICHAEL LICHTER

While Larry was a showman, he was also true to the biker form. He was a true biker and he was more concerned about being a biker than being a movie star. I think it came out of his carney background. After all, he was a star on the small stage at Coney Island. He was used to being on stage and before the public, but in the last few years of his life he got a taste of the big stage. It didn't change him one bit though; he was always the same guy. We did a lot of the *Easyriders* Bike Shows together and he was always very calm and patient with all his fans. I admired that about him.

As far as custom bike building goes, I think that if anybody had the old school style of building down, it was Larry. Because of the TV shows, he had the opportunity to build a few bikes toward the end of his life that he probably had always wanted for Larry. I took it to him and told him to give it to Bambi and tell her he missed her and bought it for her," Elisa says. "He told me, 'I can't do that. I'm not gonna say it was from me; it's from you. I'll give it to her for you.' I mean, he couldn't even have a little white lie. He wore his heart on his sleeve."

Bob Seeger Jr. first met Larry in 1995 while getting tattooed in Manhattan at a tattoo parlor called East Side Ink. "A girl who worked at East Side named Andrea did a lot of Larry's tattoo work including his neck tattoo," Bobby remembers. "The neck tattoo was still pretty fresh at the time. I had seen Larry in the magazines and in he walks. I used to see him racing his bike over bridges, through traffic, just goin' wild. A mutual friend introduced us in 1995 and Larry and I had both just stopped drinking so we started hanging out, gettin' coffee, and became friends."

While heading up Psycho Cycles, Larry was also building motors out of his apartment at the same time. "I was riding a full dresser Harley back then," Bobby laughs. "I remember showing up at Larry's place and going for rides. One time in 1996, we were riding along at like ninety miles per hour and we came over this hill and suddenly all the traffic was stopped dead. Larry just cranked on the go juice and blasted between all the traffic while I was grabbin' my brakes and trying not to get killed.

photos by MICHAEL LICHTER

to build but never had the money to do. The bikes he built were the accumulation of all the things he did over the years. He was able to express his ideas fully in the last few years of his life. Everyone always infers that they have followed Larry for the past 20 years, but the truth is, he only became really known for his bike building over his last few years. He continues to be a big influence in the custom bike world because he was a real guy.

The custom bike industry can be a dog-eat-dog world, but I've never heard of anyone who didn't like Indian Larry, and I think that can be attributed to the fact that he was so down-to-earth. When I think of Larry, I see him standing on the seat of his bike, looking straight ahead, totally focused. He always had a focused look when he surfed his bike. He had a way of being laid back and focused at the same time.

—Dave Perewitz

It's good to be King. Larry's hand-carved question mark throne.

When I finally caught up with Larry he was just laughin' like a little kid. That's how I like to remember Larry, sittin' there on his bike, gigglin' like a six-year-old who just got away with somethin'." The next time the two friends went riding, Larry had some advice for Bobby: "Leave the boat at home."

As the world entered a new millennium, Indian Larry was poised for greatness. The magazines had brought him a cult following and he was ready to open his own business. The new shop was a wonderland of custom magic known as Gasoline Alley in Brooklyn, New York.

Larry teamed up with his bike building buddy from the Psycho Cycles days, Paul Cox, and a business partner named Gerard Mortillaro (Larry and Gerard went their separate ways in 2003). Then, Larry brought in Bobby Seeger to handle their clothing line. Their early T-shirt designs just displayed an old-school iron cross with the words "Gasoline Alley" above it, and "New York City Choppers" below it. The place was very much inspired by the kustom kulture of Ed Roth, Von Dutch, Robt. Williams, and the incredible artistry in leather and iron that Paul Cox brought to the shop. They soon hired a creative Japanese kid named Keino to help build bikes, and the multi-talented Johnny Mack to weld all the one-of-a-kind tanks and fenders. Together, they were like a team of superheroes taking the custom bike world by storm.

This lead to other bike features in *Easyriders* and *The Horse* magazines. Still, fame is not the same thing as fortune, and money was always an issue. The gang at Gasoline Alley was always low on cash but high on inspiration. But Larry's creative genius and wild persona was about to be recognized by that modern miracle known as television, and the road to success was about to become a six lane superhighway!

photo by MICHAEL LICHTER

Michael Lichter was hanging out of the back of a convertible to get this shot of Paul Cox and Larry on a back road in Daytona Beach, Florida. Cruising along at about 40 miles per hour, the boys get balanced . . .

Fame and Fortune

"Larry had my respect.
Cool is cool, you know what I mean?"

PAUL YAFFE

WE have reached the stage of Larry's life in which our hero returns home from life's weary journey, triumphant!—just as Odysseus' successful return to Ithaca, or Luke blowing up the Death Star. Indian Larry was about to have his life's story splashed across the public consciousness through today's story-telling medium of television. His hero's journey was about to become public—big time. And how appropriate, for all heroes must have their legends told.

By now, you all probably know the story of how bike builder and metal maverick Jesse James has become a household name. Thom Beers' Original Productions was working on a TV series called *On The Inside* in 2000, which showed various interesting and off-beat occupations. These included an underwater welder and a rodeo clown. Producer Hugh King called and asked me to introduce him to a local Southern California motorcycle builder for an episode of the series. The builder had to be young, energetic, and wild, according to Hugh. I took him down to meet Jesse James in Long Beach, California. "See the spider web

...and stand up on their seats to surf their bikes. Larry's "signature" pose was "the Crucifix," while Paul likes to place a foot on the gas tank for a more surfer effect.

gates, the pit bulls, the shark tank?" But the jackpot was Jesse himself and the documentary of the young outlaw was called *Motorcycle Mania*, which aired on The Discovery Channel. It was the highest rated show in cable history.

As happens in TV land, success breeds sequels and for the sequel to *Motorcycle Mania*, Jesse was to build a chopper from the ground up and ride it to Sturgis for the annual Black Hills Classic Motorcycle Rally. He was allowed to bring friends on the ride and one of these was Indian Larry. "Yeah, he's sort of a stunt man," Jesse explained. "He rides his bike through a wall of fire."

Naturally, Larry being the free spirited wild child that he was, and never one to turn down an opportunity to market himself, not only appeared on *Motorcycle Mania II* in 2003, he stole the show. The shots of Larry "surfing" his bike, standing up on the seat in his now famous crucifix formation, became a part of Larry's legend. He was shown roaring down the highway reclining on his bike with his feet up on the handlebars and his head resting on the rear fender, a big smile on his face. Larry was good TV, as Hugh King told me, and a media star was born.

Certainly Larry had achieved a certain level of popularity from appearing in famous paintings and photographs in New York. He had enjoyed a modicum of success thanks to having his work in popular motorcycle magazines such as *Easyriders*, but television brought the man with the tattoos on his neck into America's living room. The success of *Motorcycle Mania II* introduced Larry to a vast new audience. People from all over the country were calling Gasoline Alley for T-shirts—proof that exposure equals retail sales.

During a ride at Daytona BikeWeek for *Easyriders* magazine. The number of people who recognized Larry was amazing—he had a wave and a smile for all of them.

photo by MICHAEL LICHTER

Original Productions was working on another idea for the Discovery Channel involving pitting two very different bike builders against each other in a race against the clock to build a custom bike and then ride the bikes to a motorcycle event somewhere. Once at the event a people's choice vote would determine the best of the two bikes and the winner would advance to another episode. The limited-episode series was to be called *The Great Biker Build-Off*, and the first episode pitted rebel Florida builder Billy Lane against upscale Arizona builder Roger Bourget (Billy won). For episode two, Indian Larry was chosen to go up against a builder who was truly his opposite.

Paul Yaffe creates sleek and original works of motorized art from his shop, Paul Yaffe Originals, in Phoenix, Arizona. While Larry likes to see every nut and bolt on his sparse creations, Paul often covers his chassis with swoopy bodywork and lavish paint schemes. If Larry's bikes remind one of the insides of a pocket watch, Paul's customs are more like a slick Ferrari. This pairing of Paul and Larry had old school against new thought, North against South, old veteran against young gun.

For Larry's entry in the build-off, he, Paul Cox, and Keino created a tribute to his mentor, Ed "Big Daddy" Roth. The Rat Fink bike (as it became known) was the perfect Indian Larry machine. Larry liked to see all the parts of the motorcycle exposed. He liked to see all the gizmos, the clockworks of the bike. The art was in the function. "I like all the

The *Biker Build-Off*'s Executive Producer, Hugh King, announces that Larry is the winner of the build off against Billy Lane.

nuts and bolts and fittings, the linkages and the mechanicalness of it. I like to see all the mechanicalness," he told the cameras.

Paul Yaffe's bike was a stretched, bright red, pro-street design called the *Phantom*, which shot 30-foot flames from its exhaust pipes. Paul figured that if Larry got up on his seat and surfed his bike, he could set him on fire with his scoot's flamethrower. At the build-off finale, held in Laconia, New Hampshire, as part of their annual Loudon Classic Bike Week, Paul Cox simulated Yaffe's flame thrower by lighting a spray can of cleaning fluid and blasting his own flames while Larry did a tire shredding burn out. Larry was very personable, talking to everyone at the event and soliciting votes. His easy manner and old school biker way stole the event. When the tire smoke cleared, Larry was the winner of the build-off and, like Jesse before him, a TV star was born.

At about this time, motorcycle show promoter John Green and I were working on an idea for our *Easyriders* Bike Shows that would involve many of the custom bike builders seen on The Great Biker Build-Off series. John agreed to bring several of these builders out to our shows to meet the public, sign autographs, take photos with fans, and show off their latest custom creations. We called it the *Easyriders* Centerfold Tour and featured such popular builders (as seen on The Discovery Channel) as Billy Lane, Eddie Trotta, Kim Suter, Kendall Johnson, and Paul Yaffe. John Green and I approached Larry and made a deal to add him to the shows, which turned out to be an enormous hit! People who visited our bike shows loved talking to Larry. No matter how mobbed he was, he always took time to speak to everyone, offer a kind word, shake hands, sign autographs, and take pictures with adoring fans. He was a man of the people who had made good and our event goers knew it. It may truly be said that Larry was adored by the masses.

photos by MICHAEL LICHTER

Larry takes to the stage and explains that the build-off was about brotherhood and that there are no winners or losers.

photos from INDIAN LARRY ARCHIVES

Larry shares the *Biker Build-Off* win with his friend and bro, Billy Lane.

Lifting the trophy before the packed crowd at the Hard Rock Casino tent in Sturgis . . .

photo by MICHAEL LICHTER

In the summer of 2003, Hugh King brought Larry and his crew back for another *Biker Build-Off* episode, this time against the winner of episode one, Billy Lane of Melbourne, Florida. Larry's metalflake root beer creation was conjured straight from the heart and Billy's wild low slung chopper was the perfect counterpart. But these two old school–bike builders had nothing but respect for each other. They even hosted a party together during the Sturgis Rally to kick off the event. Billy's Choppers Inc. and Larry's Gasoline Alley put on a helluva wing-ding and both Billy and Larry smoked the tires right off their bikes in The Full Throttle Saloon's burn out pits.

Never let it be said that Larry's bikes were not functional; if anything, they brought the level of pure functionality up a notch. After all, his bikes were designed to be ridden on the pot-holed, mean streets of New York City. While Larry's choppers were functional, they were also truly motorized pieces of art. "We definitely treat the bikes as art," Larry told the Discovery cameras. "As far as I'm concerned it is one of the highest art forms, because it combines all media: sculpture, painting, as well as all the mechanics, and it's just a lot more than any one single medium."

A story that truly shows Larry's righteous heart and soul involves the finale of the build-off against Billy Lane in Sturgis. By the narrowest of margins, Larry was voted the winner of the contest. True to his old-school roots, he took the microphone and told the gathered crowd, "There are no winners, there are no losers!" Then, he took a cutting tool and he and Billy cut the trophy into a dozen pieces, autographed each one, and gave them out to the crowd that surrounded them. Now *that*, as we say in the biker world, was showing class! It was also brilliant TV, as Hugh King can tell you.

...Larry cuts the trophy to pieces. Now that's good TV!

Larry's second *Biker Build-Off* winning bike was featured in the June 2004 issue of *Easyriders* (No. 372, pages 18 to 22). The root beer ride also made the cover, and in the biker universe, that meant that Larry had made it to the top of his game, fair and square. In the article, Larry talked about the build-off finale, "Who cares who wins? It's about building bikes and going for a ride. People have lost track of that. Too many people have forgotten what the brotherhood is all about. Billy is a good friend; we both did the best we could. He just happened to be chips down that particular day. Other days, it's me. That's all."

After the second Indian Larry episode aired on The Discovery Channel, things went nuts at Gasoline Alley. The little shop in Brooklyn buzzed with activity thanks to all the high profile publicity generated by television. But there were also clashes of personalities and Larry's partner Gerard Mortillaro left the business. Then the three motorized musketeers—Larry, Paul Cox, and Keino—really put the pedal to the metal and worked out some truly awe-inspiring custom bikes. More bikes were shot for more magazines, and Larry started another season of the *Easyriders* Centerfold Tour. Interestingly, of the builders on the tour, Larry, Billy Lane, and Paul Yaffe, were on hand at almost all of the *Easyriders* Bike Shows around the country. They were all friends and treated the public like gold. Larry was a shining star at the top of his game after a lifetime of trials and tribulations. Those were truly his glory days.

At one of the bike shows, Larry and I had a heart to heart about what he wanted to do with his life since fame and fortune had arrived. Offers flooded in for more TV shows, book deals, merchandising opportunities, and so on. But Larry's wishes were simple: he didn't want to build a production line of bikes. He just wanted to meet people, travel, have a good time, and build a few cool custom bikes. "I'm gonna build

photo from INDIAN LARRY ARCHIVES

After autographing each piece of the sawed up trophy, Larry and Billy throw the pieces to the screaming crowd.

Keino makes adjustments on *Chain of Mystery*, Larry's last ride for Discovery Channel.

Right: Riding with Mondo Porras from Denver's Choppers for Larry's last Discovery Channel *Biker Build-Off* show. Mondo says it was the ride of his life.

photos from INDIAN LARRY ARCHIVES

the bikes the way I wanna build 'em," Larry told me. "If people like 'em, that's fine, but I'm gonna build 'em for me. And I don't care if anybody buys 'em. That's not why I build 'em. I've still got a lot of ideas in my head, so many that I know I'll never get them all from inside my brain to rolling down the road, but I like a challenge."

Larry looked into my eyes and said, "I've been waiting for this shot my whole life. I always knew I had what it takes. I just had to be at the right place at the right time. Now I'm not gonna blow it, and I'm not gonna forget what it's all really about. I'm still gonna live every moment to the fullest. I'm gonna take the time to be in the moment and do what I love most—ride."

Driving NASCAR race cars with (left to right) master bike builders Kendall Johnson, Dave Perewitz and Billy Lane. contributed by BAMBI

Legends Never Die

"Tell me muse, of the man of many ways..."
THE ODYSSEY

AT the end of the hero's journey, if he survives life's ordeals, the hero is often granted his own divination. Intrinsically, it is the expansion of consciousness and of being (illumination); the final work is that of the return. If the powers have blessed the hero, he sets forth under the protection of the gods. The hero emerges (resurrection) radiant, and restores the world. In the case of Indian Larry, our hero traveled far and overcame some of life's most intense trials, learning many life lessons in the process. Many of his friends might tell you that after Larry was redeemed by the gods, they chose to pluck him from this world to be offered greater rewards.

In many modern myths, the hero's return includes his own death and transition to another, better world. This concept is also a part of the legends of many lands and times, including the Viking's belief in Valhalla, the Christian belief in a heavenly reward, and even the New Age concept of life after death in other planes of existence or other dimensions.

Death is simply the doorway to a new dimension of infinite possibility for the hero, and to those who remain on the Earthly

If it had two wheels, Larry loved it. This is actually Bambi's bike. contributed by BAMBI

The Coney Island Polar Bear Club. contributed by BAMBI

Angel wings were added to Larry's question mark after he died. The winged question mark is now the Indian Larry Legacy logo. photo by MICHAEL LICHTER

Goth Girl sports question mark dermagraphics on her left arm. She made the trip all the way from San Francisco to honor Larry.

photo by MICHAEL LICHTER

realm, the hero becomes an inspiration with incredible power to change lives. So it has been with Larry DeSmedt.

In the summer of 2004, Indian Larry was riding high on the success he waited a lifetime to obtain. As the reigning champion of the *Biker Build-Off*, he began working on his third *Build-Off* bike, this time going up against the Godfather of Choppers, Mondo Porras of Denver's Choppers, Henderson, Nevada. Larry, Paul Cox, and Keino were building their wildest bike ever, known as the *Chain of Mystery*. This amazing motorcycle's frame was made out of heavy tow chain that was welded into a solid rigid motorcycle frame. Larry had no idea if the chain would hold, but he was sure going to give it a hell of a try.

The *Chain of Mystery* chopper was finished on time, in just 10 days. Larry and his crew rode with Mondo on his old school digger-style chopper through the lush North Carolina countryside on their way to the grand finale of the *Build-Off*—Larry's chain frame held together very well. Mondo said the ride was the best one he ever had. "Riding handlebar to handlebar with Larry was an incredible experience," Mondo said. "It was all I could do to keep up." As always, Larry was living life to the fullest. Every moment was a perfect and serene moment, there was only *now* for this mystical biker shaman.

Like Zorro's "Z," you never know where the sign of Larry will show up.

photos by MICHAEL LICHTER

Above: Larry rides on Chris' shoulder . . . always. Right: Master bike builder Kendall Johnson shows off his skin art tribute to Larry.

The street was packed on North 14th in Brooklyn. Everybody who knew Larry would tell you he would have loved a party like this. photo by MICHAEL LICHTER

Original Productions cameras were on hand to record the day for posterity. The footage was used in a tribute to Larry on The Discovery Channel.

MONDO PORRAS
Denver's Choppers, Henderson, Nevada

I had heard of Larry and seen him in the motorcycle magazines over the years but I first met him in person during the filming of *Motorcycle Mania II*. Jesse James and Larry stopped at my shop, Denver's Choppers, in Henderson, Nevada, on their way to Sturgis. Larry needed a magneto for his bike. I remember walking out and looking at his chopper and I got goose bumps on the spot. In fact, they left that part in the show.

I liked Larry right away because he was an old timer and easy for me to relate to. He was an East-Coast old-school guy

Hugh King (far left) joins the Indian Larry crew to say a few words on a day when no words were enough.

At one point Larry pulled over to look at a pristine stream running next to the road. "Let's go skinny-dipping," he yelled and stripped off his clothes. A few other brave souls followed him into the shallow water, whooping like little kids. Soon, the TV crew and the bikers were back on the road and arrived in Concord, North Carolina, to take part in the Liquid Steel Motorcycle Show. Event-goers poured into the show to ogle Mondo and Larry's Discovery Channel creations.

On Saturday, August 28, 2004, the spectators voted to decide the winner of the *Build-Off* and Larry was performing daredevil stunts for the crowd outside. He rode his stunt bike through a wall of flames, and topped this off with some of his famous motorcycle stunts, including his signature bike surfing bit, standing up on the seat, his arms stretched out in the classic crucifix pose. But something was wrong. The bike was

photos by MICHAEL LICHTER

and I'm a West-Coast old-school guy, so we could relate to each other. We didn't have any CNC machines, just old school bike building. You could say that we had both been through the ranks and we didn't build bikes for fame and fortune; we did it because we were bikers. When it came to all the TV cameras and getting to be famous for building bikes, Larry would just say, "What's this all about? I'm just me."

Another thing I liked about Larry was that you knew exactly where he was coming from. He was the real deal. If he looked you in the eye and promised you something, he was good for it. That's a rare thing these days.

One of my favorite times spent with Larry was when we were in Hawaii for a bike show about two months before he died. One day, he and I were all by ourselves, swimming in the ocean with turtles on the north shore. I remember him talking about his philosophies on life. Basically, he was all about living the simple life. Larry saw life as a great gift and was just happy to be here, experiencing it to the fullest.

When I think of Larry, I see him jamming down the road on one of his bikes, with a big, contented grin on his face. It's funny; he always wore sweatpants when he rode because he was more comfortable that way. Larry was a dude who was very comfortable in his own skin.

What impressed me most about Larry was the purity of the man. He lived the biker lifestyle and would give you the shirt off his back if you needed it. There was a time when if someone was broken down by the side of the road, you helped him get going and never charged him a dime. That's what the biker going too slow, no more than 30 miles per hour, and the front end began to wobble badly. Instead of leaning forward to grab the handlebars and then sitting back down in the saddle, as he might usually do, Larry fell backward off the bike and hit his head on the asphalt.

There was a collective gasp . . . and then silence. Everyone expected Larry to get back up. When he didn't, friends and crew ran to his side. He was airlifted to the hospital immediately. I was supposed to be at the taping of the *Build-Off* episode with Larry but was attending a dealer meeting. I can still hear Billy Lane's voice on the other end of my cell phone when he called me early on Sunday morning. "Larry fell off his bike and they don't know if he's gonna make it." Mondo called minutes later and gave me more details. He and Billy, as well as Kendall Johnson, Paul Cox, Keino, and Bambi, were all at the hospital.

My mind was reeling. How could this be? Larry had performed that stunt thousands of times. He knew what he was doing. How could this happen? On Monday, August 30, the man known as Indian Larry slipped out of this world.

No one in the motorcycle industry could believe that Larry was gone. He was more alive than any 100 of the walking dead suits out there on the streets. Writing of his passing in *Easyriders* was one of the hardest

photos by MICHAEL LICHTER

brotherhood is all about and that is what Larry was all about.

You know, from watching him on TV, I think a lot of people want to be like Larry. I think he humbled a lot of people because he was so real and genuine. He also had so much love for his crew. They were family through thick and thin. The one thing he said to me that I'll never forget is that he didn't want to do the stunt that killed him. He didn't want to do it that day but was pressured into doing it by the promoter of the event. Larry was the consummate showman, so I guess the show had to go on.

The one thing I will take to my grave is Larry's last ride. He and I were blasting through the Blue Ridge Mountains parkway, handlebar to handlebar, sparks flying, burning through the turns at high speed, neck and neck, just jamming. You form a real kinship and a bond with someone when you ride hard, inches from them at high speed. You have each other's lives in your hands, and I had total trust in Larry; he was the master. That's what being a biker is all about. I think he was the purest form of motorcycle rider. It was an honor and a privilege to ride with him, and keep up with Larry. That last ride was truly a spiritual experience. I would ride through the gates of Hell with that guy.

—*Mondo Porras*

Big Chris, Jose from Puerto Rico, and Bobby Seeger during Daytona BikeWeek.

Keino with Chica of Chica's Custom Cycles, in Huntington Beach, California. Keino used to wear a T-shirt that proclaimed, "I am not Chica."

Elisa and Bobby Seeger at the 2004 Laconia Rally. Along with Paul Cox and Keino, they are keeping the legend alive at Indian Larry Legacy.

Loving mementos line the sidewalks. On a nearby brick wall, spray painted graffiti proclaims, "Do a burnout for Larry!"

right page photos by MICHAEL LICHTER

Grinder Girl throws a little "performance art" at the masses during Larry's memorial party.

photo by NORMAN BLAKE

things I have ever done. Indian Larry died at 55 years old and had only experienced the victory of life without drugs, the love of Bambi, and the success and fame he deserved for a short six years. He was larger than life and a man of extremes. Some say he was taken from us because the gods wanted a chopper. Knowing Larry, that is entirely possible.

"I think if God rode a bike, I feel like he would ride a Harley-Davidson chopper," Larry said on one of The Discovery Channel shows. "On the right bike, on the right day, and the right road, I just pretty much feel one with the universe. When I feel like I don't fit in anywhere, or I'm lonely, or I'm like, all screwed up in the head, I get on my bike and I go for a ride, and all of a sudden . . . life fits." But life didn't fit very well for those of us who knew Larry and were left behind to mourn his passing to Valhalla.

On the day of the memorial party, the question mark still hung over Brooklyn.

Larry's ashes are inside this Panhead jug, making the perfect urn for the shaman biker. photo by NORMAN BLAKE

The hand engraving was done by Larry's friend, C. J. Allen.

photos by TINA DeSMEDT-WELLS

The team from Indian Larry Legacy received a standing ovation.

In September 2004, Larry's crew held a massive street party to honor Larry. Bike builders and friends flew in from everywhere and celebrated Larry's life with the sound of Harley thunder and the smoke of burning tires. It was a helluva sendoff. On the brick wall outside the shop to this day, spray painted words read, "Do a burnout for Larry."

Larry touched and inspired thousands of people who he never met during his lifetime. Those who watched him on TV were blown away by his untimely death. Many began sending in letters, cards, gifts, and photos of the tributes they offered to Bambi and the crew at the shop. Some even tattooed their bodies with Larry's likeness, or his enigmatic question mark logo. Others dedicated their lives to living in the present as Larry had done; still others decided to live their dreams and ride and build bikes for a living. Though the loss of Indian Larry was a stunning blow to many, those who knew Larry best would say that he went out of this world the way he would have wanted to: on his motorcycle, with the wind in his face and the crowd cheering. We should all be so lucky.

"I feel you should be doing exactly what you want to do in life, how you want to do it, when you want to do it," Larry said during one of the *Build-Offs*. "Otherwise, you're wasting your life and wasting the talents that were given to you. Life is like a real precious, short gift."

The producers at Original Productions found themselves with a sizable dilemma, namely, how to present the *Build-Off* episode in which Larry died. They shelved the episode for awhile, trying to figure out how

photos by MICHAEL LICHTER

The Discovery Channel's *Biker Build-Off* finale was called *The Ultimate Chop* and featured a touching tribute to Larry.

Keino, Bambi, and Paul accept the award for Larry.

Bobby and Elisa with Billy Lane at *The Ultimate Chop* awards dinner.

Johnny Mack hanging at the *Biker Build-Off* award ceremony in Vegas.

to edit it all together in a way that would pay tribute to their fallen hero. In the end, Indian Larry was announced as the winner of that episode at the memorial, and is the all-time reigning champion. In time, Hugh King and Thom Beers put together a touching tribute program in which master bike builders Billy Lane and Kendall Johnson joined Paul Cox and Keino to build a tribute bike for Larry.

The wild purple Panhead they fashioned is called *Love Zombie*, which was a motorcycle Larry had wanted to build for he and Bambi, but never got a chance to. The four builders created a true work of motorized art and *Love Zombie* also acted as the first of many incredible bikes that the team from Larry's shop keeps building. Each motorcycle is a roaring tribute to Larry. In fact, Bobby and Elisa Seeger, Paul, Keino, Johnny Mack, and the rest of the crew have renamed the shop Indian Larry Legacy and continue where Larry left off, creating amazing,

Elisa, Johnny Mack, and Bambi at The Discovery Channel taping of *The Ultimate Chop*. It was like the Academy Awards of bike building.

photos by MICHAEL LICHTER

one-of-a-kind creations that our hero would have been proud of. "He had a vision as a sculptor, creating a chalice, creating this object of sacred artistic integrity," Bambi says, and the men and women of Indian Larry Legacy keep that vision alive and well out of their brick building at 151 North 14th Street in Brooklyn, New York. Everything in the shop is just as Larry left it. When there, you half expect to hear his flip-flops on the cement floor and see him clowning around.

And yes, a question mark still hangs out front; an iron testament to the man, the myth, and the legend of Indian Larry. It reminds us that we all live a hero's journey. We all struggle and fail sometimes. We all reach, and wonder, and dance in the dark. We are all kings and queens, fools and thieves, warriors and wizards, lovers and losers. We are all capable of greatness that can change the world. We *are* the hero with a thousand faces. We are Indian Larry . . . and the mystery continues.

Love Zombie, the Indian Larry tribute bike seen in The Discovery Channel special with its creators, (left to right) Billy Lane, Paul Cox, Kendall Johnson, and Keino.

photo by T-BEAR

LOVE ZOMBIE

This one-of-a-kind motorcycle was built as a tribute to Larry after he died. The Discovery Channel documented the build on a special one-hour-long tribute program to Larry. *Love Zombie*, as Paul Cox named this chopper, was built by Larry's friends from the *Biker Build-Off* TV series: motor wizard Kendall Johnson, master builder Billy Lane, as well as the Indian Larry Legacy crew, Paul Cox and Keino. The bike is a statement of their love and a dedication to their friend that will last forever.

LEATHER: Paul Cox hand-tooled the leather seat, featuring the Indian Larry Legacy logo.

FABRICATION: Billy Lane hand-fabricated the gas tank to fit this antique Pontiac hood ornament. Paul and Keino made this "B" inside a heart to signify Bambi's love for Larry and incorporated it on the sissy bar.

photos by MICHAEL LICHTER

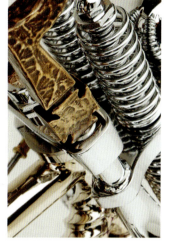

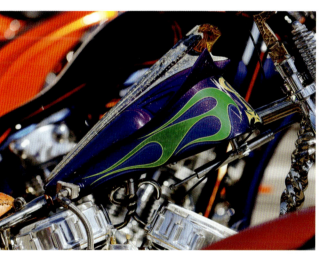

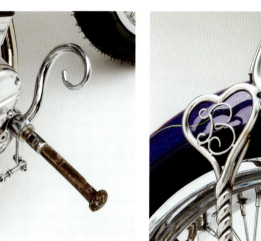

photos by MICHAEL LICHTER

Paul and Keino ride on new Indian Larry Legacy custom bikes of their own design.

Larry might not be with us in body, but he'll always be riding with us in spirit.

Johnny Mack, fabricator and welder at Indian Larry Legacy, at Daytona BikeWeek 2005.

photos by MICHAEL LICHTER

6th Street Specials, 70
Addams Family, The, 20
Allen, C. J., 89
American Dream Machine, 69
Anima mundi, 44
Bear Butte, South Dakota, 68
Beatnik Bandit, 19
Beers, Thom, 139, 143, 170
Bellevue Mental Hospital, 107, 109
Belly of the Beast tattoo joint, 126
Berserker, 78, 79
Big Chris, 60
Biker Build-Off, 35, 45, 50, 54, 64, 75, 85, 89, 104, 105, 124, 129, 132, 144, 146, 147, 149, 150, 155, 161, 162, 168, 169, 172
Biketoberfest, 55
Black Hills Classic Motorcycle Rally, 141
Bourget, Roger, 143
Brando, Marlon, 22
Brooklyn Beatnik, 94, 95
Brucker, Jim, 35
California Cruiser, 33
Cambridge, Andrea "Bambi," 52, 57, 60, 64, 81, 109, 111, 114, 116, 119–123, 132–134, 153, 162, 164, 169, 171, 172
Camel Roadhouse, 30
Campbell, Joseph, 9, 13, 40, 101
Candy Wagon, The, 54
Cassato Airbrush, 73
Chain of Mystery, 88–91, 150, 155
Chica, 60, 163
Chica's Custom Cycles, 163
Choppers Inc., 85, 130, 147
Choppers magazine, 35, 75
CNC machines, 161
Coney Island, 29, 47, 101, 105, 117, 122, 108, 130, 132, 133
Coney Island Mermaid Parade, 109
Coney Island Tattoo and Motorcycle Show, 101, 119

Cox, Paul, 31, 50, 56, 59, 60, 62, 64, 67–70, 73, 79, 81, 85, 92, 94, 117, 119, 125, 136, 138, 141, 143, 144, 149, 155, 162, 163, 169, 172, 176
Crazy Horse, 69
Cycle Fabrications, 132
D.I.L.L.I.G.A.F.'s, 69
Daddy-O, 74–77, 129
Daytona BikeWeek, 44, 60, 62, 143, 177

"THE CRUCIFIX"

Denver's Choppers, 89, 150, 155, 160
DeSmedt, Augustine, 19, 20
DeSmedt, Diane, 19, 20, 30, 32, 38, 40, 42
DeSmedt, Dorothy, 19, 20
Druid Princess, 19
Eak the Geek, 101
Earl the Eel, 12
East Side Ink, 134
Easy Rider, 30, 32
Easyriders Bike Show, 31, 32, 73, 81, 130, 133, 144
Easyriders Bike Show Centerfold Tour, 54, 81, 94, 144, 149
Easyriders magazine, 38, 73, 75, 99, 101, 119, 125, 126, 130, 136, 141, 149, 162
Editor's Choice Award, 73, 130
English Don, 130
Entelechy, 10
Fonda, Peter, 30, 32
Fredella, Nick, 130
Full Throttle Saloon, The, 31, 67, 147
Gasoline Alley, 50, 104, 136, 141, 147, 149
Grease Monkey, 72, 73, 119, 123, 130
Great Biker Build-Off, The, 143, 144
Green, John, 144
Haight-Ashbury, 38
Hard Rock Casino, Sturgis, 146
Harley-Davidson, 51, 60, 134, 164, 168

Heinz, Stag Von, 126
Hero and the Goddess, The, 11, 49
Hero with A Thousand Faces, 9
Hollister Riot, 22
Hopper, Dennis, 30, 32
Horse, The, 125, 130, 136
Hot Dog Rod, 126
Houston, Dr. Jean, 11, 49, 102
Howard, Kenneth, 30
I Was a Teenaged Werewolf, 20
Ice Cream Man from Hell, 102
Indian Larry Flying Circus, 108
Indian Larry Legacy, 92, 96, 154, 163, 168, 170–172, 176, 177
Iron Horse, 69
It Conquers the World, 20
James, Jesse, 54, 132, 139, 160
Johnny Chop, 60
Johnny Mack, 136, 169, 171, 177
Johnson, Kendall, 144, 150, 156, 162, 170, 172
Journey Museum, The, 96
Jump Time, 102
Kate, 114, 117
Keino, 50, 94, 136, 143, 149, 150, 155, 162, 163, 169, 170, 172, 176
Kent State University, 25, 32
King, Hugh, 64, 139, 141, 144, 147, 161, 170
Kramer, Stanley, 22
Laconia Bike Week, 132
Laconia Rally, 129, 163
Lane, Billy, 30–32, 54, 64, 67, 70, 85, 130, 143, 144, 147, 149, 150, 162, 170–172
Laughlin River Run, 13
Le Morte D'Arthur, 52
Leary, Timothy, 25
Lichter, Michael, 96, 138
Liquid Steel Motorcycle Show, 89, 161
Loudon Classic Bike Week, 144
Love Zombie, 93, 170, 172–175
Malory, Sir Thomas, 51
Mann, David, 68
Maplethorpe, Robert, 60
Marvin, Lee, 22
Matrix, The, 12, 49
Mitchell, Russell, 37
Monster Garage series, 126
Morgan, Sam, 18
Mortillaro, Gerard, 149
Motorcycle Mania I, 54, 132, 141
Motorcycle Mania II, 141, 160
Movieworld Cars of the Stars and Planes of Fame, 35
Mr. Tiki's Shop Droppings, 80–83
Mysterion, 19
NASCAR, 150
Nicky Boots, 67, 130
Orbitron, 19
Original Productions, 139, 143, 160, 168

Osiris, 49
Pain, 29, 102
Panhead, 60, 73, 89, 166
Paul Yaffe Originals, 143
Perewitz, Dave, 132, 133, 134, 150
Phantom, 144
Polar Bear Club, 35, 47, 104, 105
Porras, Mondo, 89, 150, 155, 160–162, 170
Poseidon, 38
Pradke, Robert, 50, 81, 89, 93
Psycho Cycles, 50, 70, 125, 126, 134
Psycho Frank, 126
Question mark, 15, 57, 93, 102, 136, 164
Rat Fink, 20, 75, 105, 143
Red Rock East Saloon, 126
Revell Corporation, 19, 32, 35
Road Agent, 19
Rotar, 19
Roth, Ed "Big Daddy," 19, 20, 29, 32, 33, 35, 54, 75, 94, 136, 143
Rotten, Rhett, 19
S&S Cycle, 92
Seeger, Bobby, 56, 132, 134, 136, 163, 170
Seeger, Elisa, 132–134, 163, 170, 171
Segle, Walt, 126
Shovelhead, 85, 93, 125
Sideshows by the Seashore Freak Show, 124
Sing Sing Prison, 42, 47
Springer, 94
Steniway's, 69
Sturgis, 30, 31, 54, 64, 67, 70, 85, 96, 146, 147, 160
Surf Fink, 20
Suter, Kim, 144
Tempting Fate, 96, 97
Testor's paint, 19
Thunder Cycle, 54
Trader Vic's, 81
Triumph, 126
Trotta, Eddie, 54, 55, 144
University of Hell, 101, 113
Von Dutch, 30, 33, 35, 81, 136
V-Twin magazine, 101
Wall of Death, 18, 19
Warhol, Andy, 60
Wells (DeSmedt), Tina, 19, 22, 32, 42, 48, 56, 64, 109
Whip's, 69
White, Timothy, 17
Wild Child, 84–87
Wild One, The, 22
Williams, Robert, 30, 35, 136
Woodstock, 30
Yaffe, Paul, 75, 104–106, 124, 132, 139, 143, 144, 149
Zarathustra's Revenge, 92, 93